Food Service Management

How to Succeed in the High-Risk Restaurant Business —

By Someone Who Did

By Bill Wentz

THE COMPLETE GUIDE TO FOOD SERVICE MANAGEMENT: HOW TO SUCCEED IN THE HIGH RISK RESTAURANT BUSINESS — BY SOMEONE WHO DID

ISBN-13: 978-1-60138-024-1   ISBN-10: 1-60138-024-0

Library of Congress Cataloging-in-Publication Data

Wentz, William J., 1933-
Food service management: how to succeed in the high-risk restaurant
business: by someone who did/by William J. Wentz.
   p. cm.
ISBN-13: 978-1-60138-024-1 (alk. paper)
ISBN-10: 1-60138-024-0 (alk. paper)
   1. Food service management--United States. 2. Restaurant
management--United States. 3. Restaurants--Vocational guidance--United
States. I. Title.

TX911.3.M27W435 2008
647.95068--dc22
      2007044786

INTERIOR LAYOUT DESIGN: Vickie Taylor • vtaylor@atlantic-pub.com
PROOFREADER: Cathy Bernardy • bernardyjones@gmail.com

Printed in the United States

Printed on Recycled Paper

We recently lost our beloved pet "Bear," who was not only our best and dearest friend, but also the "Vice President of Sunshine" here at Atlantic Publishing. He did not receive a salary but worked tirelessly 24 hours a day to please his parents. Bear was a rescue dog that turned around and showered myself, my wife Sherri, his grandparents Jean, Bob, and Nancy and every person and animal he met (maybe not rabbits) with friendship and love. He made a lot of people smile every day.

We wanted you to know that a portion of the profits of this book will be donated to The Humane Society of the United States.

— Douglas & Sherri Brown

THE HUMANE SOCIETY
OF THE UNITED STATES©

The human-animal bond is as old as human history. We cherish our animal companions for their unconditional affection and acceptance. We feel a thrill when we glimpse wild creatures in their natural habitat or in our own backyard.

Unfortunately, the human-animal bond has at times been weakened. Humans have exploited some animal species to the point of extinction.

The Humane Society of the United States makes a difference in the lives of animals here at home and worldwide. The HSUS is dedicated to creating a world where our relationship with animals is guided by compassion. We seek a truly humane society in which animals are respected for their intrinsic value, and where the human-animal bond is strong.

Want to help animals? We have plenty of suggestions. Adopt a pet from a local shelter, or join The Humane Society and be a part of our work to help companion animals and wildlife. You will be funding our educational, legislative, investigative, and outreach projects in the United States and across the globe.

Or perhaps you'd like to make a memorial donation in honor of a pet, friend, or relative? You can through our Kindred Spirits program. If you'd like to contribute in a more structured way, our Planned Giving Office has suggestions about estate planning, annuities, and even gifts of stock that avoid capital gains taxes.

Maybe you have land that you would like to preserve as a lasting habitat for wildlife. Our Wildlife Land Trust can help you. Perhaps the land you want to share is a backyard — that's enough. Our Urban Wildlife Sanctuary Program will show you how to create a habitat for your wild neighbors.

So you see, it's easy to help animals. The HSUS is here to help.

The Humane Society of the United States
2100 L Street NW
Washington, DC 20037
202-452-1100
www.hsus.org

Author Dedication

In memory of my long-term mentor and friend,

Clarence E. Koester

Table of

Contents

Food Cost...49

Chapter 4: Labor Cost Control...............................65

Chapter 5: The Other Costs...77

Foreword

By John R. Farquharson

This is a book about survival in one of the most competitive and risky businesses in the world, to say nothing about the extraordinary demand for a person's high energy, for infinite knowledge, and for doing the right thing most of the time. For anyone currently in the industry or who may be contemplating food service as a career, this read will spell out — quite vividly — the key factors necessary to succeed, in common-sense terms. Bill Wentz speaks plainly with a knowledge drawn from practical experiences of what works best in managing this crazy but wonderful business. The emphasis is on setting the right priorities and spending, or rather investing, your time and effort wisely. Wentz outlines clear steps and advice on most every aspect of building your business, controlling your costs, developing great employees who clearly understand what you mean, and, most important, keeping your customers happy and loyal.

Food service is a demanding career, but it can also be a fun business if you are in the groove. This means being comfortable and having full confidence in your abilities and being well-prepared to deal with everyday problems. Life in this business can be exciting and fulfilling, and if you follow a sensible plan, there is no reason why you cannot enjoy a fair balance between your career and your personal life. It is up to you and every individual to make it work. Due to the diverse and different training backgrounds of food service people, everyone does it a little bit differently. That is good because it reflects creativity and produces a variety of food services the consumer seeks out and enjoys.

Career-focused individuals who are the best prepared and who apply the sound fundamentals of basic management practices seem to be those special managers who build the most successful and enduring businesses. Those are the "Star Managers" every company and business enterprise is looking for — special people who make things work without constant supervision, solve problems on their own, and create great services for their customers. Whenever we have conducted a training seminar in food service management it seems we often were reinforcing the importance of the basic fundamentals. We spoke of these as going "back to basics." Without living it and every day applying the true basics of sound management, all the advertising gimmicks and special promotions attempted will not cure the ills of an unsound food service operation.

In this book you will learn about the basics and then some. Prepare yourself well, and I recommend learning from a professional who has been there and done that. If you do not know what makes this business tick, you are in trouble. And if you do not know what you do not know, it is even worse. Do it right, study the basic principles of good food service management, and you are well on your way to a successful and happy career.

John R. Farquharson
President, International Food Safety Council
and Executive Emeritus ARAMARK Corporation

John Farquharson grew up in the food service business. His family owned a resort in Maine where he learned about the industry from a young age — washing dishes, pots, and pans; tending a garden for produce for the table; mopping floors; and cleaning out grease traps.

He attended college at the University of Denver School of Hotel and Restaurant Management, where he earned a Bachelor's of Science Degree in Business Administration and was designated Athlete of the Year by the Sigma Chi Fraternity. He was honored as the University of Denver's Alumnus of the Year. John also attended the Harvard Graduate School of Business and served as a fund agent for them for many years. He has received Honorary Doctorates from the University of Denver, Johnson & Wales University, and The Culinary Institute of America.

He is a past chairman of the National Restaurant Association; past chairman and trustee emeriti of the Educational Foundation of the National Restaurant Association; chairman emeritus of the National Automatic Merchandising Association; director emeriti of the Culinary Institute of America; past chairman of the Philadelphia Crime Commission; director of Philadelphia March of Dimes; director of Delaware Valley Easter Seal Society; trustee of Westbrook College in Portland, Maine; and a fund agent for the Harvard Graduate School of Business. He also served on the USDA Research, Extension, Education, and Economics Advisory Board.

John is the winner of the Multi Unit Food Service Operator (MUFSO) Operator of the Year Award, the IFMA Silver Plate Operator of the Year Award, Nation's Restaurant News Pioneer Award, and, most recently, the Thad & Alice Eure Ambassador of Hospitality Award.

John enjoyed a 40-year career with ARAMARK. He was president of ARAMARK food service for 15 years, then chairman of its global food services, and retired as Executive Emeritus. He joined the National

Restaurant Association team as president of the International Food Safety council — an organization he founded when he was doing his one-year stint as the voluntary Chairman of the National Restaurant Association.

He is dedicated to the council's mission of "heightening the awareness of the importance of food safety education." He travels the country and the world speaking on behalf of food safety and proper food handling techniques.

Introduction

Trying how to figure out what to do for the rest of your life is perplexing for just about everyone. It does not matter if you are still in school, just starting out on the job, or reflecting seriously on your situation well into your career. The more we read, attend career seminars, and listen to well-intentioned advice from family and friends, the more confusing it becomes. So many choices and so little time. Sometimes we wish we had more than just one life so we could pursue any number of interesting vocations. It even presents a bigger puzzle to resolve when we possess a preponderance of high energy and have a strong need to excel.

Many proponents advise people to find out what they love to do and then to pursue that dream with all their heart and soul. That is well and good, but I've known few people who were that firmly decided on what they love to do. Playing a musical instrument may be enjoyable, but if one does not excel at it and is unwilling to practice, it will hardly sustain a flourishing career. It has to be more than just a passing fancy or a pleasurable pastime. Most discover their true interests from the variety of subjects they take in school, from the people they admire, and from working in different kinds of part-time jobs. Some discover their dreams by accident, some by necessity, and perhaps even one or two by plan.

Many young people get their first introduction to food service from the many ground-level positions easily available to them. It is usually a part-time job strictly for extra income, with little intention of pursuing it as a vocation. A few get turned on by the fast pace, the joy of working with food, and the fun of interacting with a variety of people. These early experiences, if they are good ones, motivate some of these young people to begin thinking enthusiastically about food service as a possible career. These upbeat individuals could become superb candidates for a food service company, but not many are persuaded to pursue the idea further. Other career options by comparison suddenly begin to appear more attractive. It is an industry problem, because the field of food service has not done a good job of reaching out and selling itself. There are many excellent, well-paying opportunities for those with ambition, and the industry needs to recruit them with a greater effort. By doing so it wouldn't have to contend with the management shortages it struggles with today. It takes some extra work since food service as a career does not compete well with other vocations, which are perceived as more prestigious and more financially rewarding.

Because of limited interest, the numerous professional career openings do not receive their fair share of attention, and the recruiting needs of the field remain unfulfilled. However, critical personnel shortages create some excellent opportunities for those who wish to investigate and learn more about where to look and whom to contact. A concerted effort can be a golden opportunity for those seeking career opportunities in the food service industry.

The field of food service management is much broader and more diverse than most people realize, and managers hold well-paying positions. These jobs require people who understand the sound fundamentals of food preparation, appreciate the value of personal service, and most important, possess good people skills.

It has been my good fortune to have found and enjoyed a rewarding career in the world of food service management. It was not so much by plan, because at the time I had a limited view of what was out there. Opportunities were primarily slanted toward the major hotel and restaurant chains that were prevalent during that time. Recruiters from those same firms also had a strong influence in directing graduating students on their choice of careers. Good as that all was, they didn't get into the specifics of what those jobs entailed and where they were headed. Of course, during that whirlwind period, getting a job, any job was of primary importance. I believe the contents of this book should provide the reader some further enlightenment about the finer points. Learn about the details and help yourself make a better long-term decision from the start.

During the early stages of my career as a management trainee with a major food service management company, it was simply a matter of learning what to do and then applying myself. The business of contract management services was rapidly growing, and early success seemed to come easily. As I advanced into larger responsibilities, I then became responsible for the food service managers who directed our operations on the front line. Now the fact was my continued growth and success depended more on their operating results rather than just my own. By comparison, it seemed easy when only I had to carry the ball and it was my decisions and actions alone that were the main basis for achieving results. Before, I had only to depend on myself. But things changed, and it was a whole new ball game. The most difficult realization was that many managers did not share my zeal nor have the education or training I was privileged to acquire from the beginning.

It was not until much later that I realized how lucky I was to have had the direction and guidance from experienced mentors who helped me along from the start. The people I had worked for were old pros who had grown up in the industry from the ground up. Many of my former supervisory managers received their food service training during military service or grew up learning their skills by working in a variety of kitchens. Some advanced further and became accomplished chefs. Each one, at the time, was a "food person" who was willing to share their experience and knowledge with the new, up-and-coming managers. It was, for me and others, a great period for developing and formulating professional standards.

As times changed, it was taken for granted that all new management personnel would be developed along the same lines, but that was not the case. As the old managers retired, a new management style appeared. The business was becoming more sophisticated. Public relations, marketing, and client communications required a more educated, liberal arts type of background. Managers were selected based on their ability to communicate, their formal education, and the image they presented. It was important for the company to grow along with the industry and be able to relate to a more demanding clientele. It was the right move for the changing times, but something was lost along the way.

The new breed, though effective in their own right, seemed to lack some of the skills for managing food services that was attributable to the old guard. The new managers were good but were limited when it came to their knowledge of food production and quality control. Food service standards gradually fell from the level they had been in the past, and often their new client relations skills were not enough to overcome some serious food service deficiencies.

As time went on, especially after losing some valuable accounts to the competition, companies began to fill gaps with technical support. Trained food production managers and professional chefs were hired to supplement a manager's lack of food expertise to improve performance. Finally, it was realized that a single manager could not provide all the answers. It now takes more of a team of specialists to meet the challenges in an increasingly demanding marketplace. Still, due to time and money restraints, many new managers coming into the industry are not provided with the intensive training and guidance required to be fully competent. It takes good front-line management to make the right things happen, but unfortunately, some of the most respected food service companies give short change to this critical human resource. For one reason or another, they get off track and forget it takes two most important things for their business to succeed: attracting more bright people into the industry and giving them the best training possible. Many good things have been done, but there is still a long way to go.

Food service employers may not always be able to hire skilled employees with great attitudes that match their own. They must first come to the realization that it is their responsibility to initiate the building of positive attitudes within their workforce, because in the real world it doesn't come ready made. Someone has to bring together the right ingredients for the recipe and mix well before the cake goes in the oven. Employers must believe that everyone wants to be inspired by something and that you can't inspire people if you don't communicate. Food service is essentially a person-to-person business that can flourish only when it is built on positive attitudes and respecting each individual's sense of self-worth. This is where the responsibility of corporate leadership comes into play, and it must set a good example from the top. By treating people with respect and dignity at all levels, managers demonstrate the right attitude that should be practiced by everyone in the organization. They should know above all that skilled managers with great attitudes are fundamental for determining business success.

Reflecting on these concerns for an industry that has given me so much, I thought I should give something back by sharing my experiences and a few lessons I have learned along the way. In these chapters you will find some ideas and a philosophy of doing business that has worked well for me. Some I have been taught by others, and some I have learned through trial and error. Not everyone shares all of my views or will agree with my preferred management style, and that's because this is a unique industry with diverse opinions about almost everything. I can guarantee that whenever two or three food service professionals get together there will surely emerge a few engaging debates. It's a never-ending learning process for those who wish to continue growing, so it's good to have an open mind and welcome different ideas. Here you will find some fundamentals about food service management that should be an essential part of your knowledge, and perhaps you will even discover a few gems of wisdom to help you along the way.

Chapter 1

Where to Begin?

"Take responsibility for a million-dollar food service operation within the first two years of employment. Develop into an executive director of food operations and have a full range of opportunity for personal creativity and growth. We are looking for ambitious people with a strong desire to be in charge. Join our winning team and build a rewarding future for yourself."

Doesn't that sound like an ad you might think worthy of further investigation? If you are looking for a career that offers early responsibility and the opportunity to express your individuality, then certainly take a strong look at the food service industry. Food service is a diversified and growing industry with an extraordinarily heavy demand for qualified management. Perusing the employment section of trade magazines and local newspapers reveals a wide variety of job positions waiting to be filled. Recruiting good food service people is a major function within all food service companies. It is the lifeblood of their organization, and those who do it the best are the most likely to be the most successful. It is much the same for an athletic coach who needs to keep recruiting new talent so his team continues to win. Next to sports, there is hardly an industry that depends more on human power than food service.

The opportunities are virtually unlimited, but determining the right road to take can be a difficult one. But before choosing a path, first decide which is the one that will take you where you want to go. Much depends on your outlook and what is most desirable to you. Deciding on a goal is the first step. Whether just starting out or considering a career change, your goals need to be clearly put down in writing. Merely thinking about a change is not enough.

It is also important to commit to writing what kind of life style is desired and what it is about certain aspects of food service that will allow you to enjoy that life style. This will take some soul searching and the preparation of many "pro and con" lists. It is an exercise worth doing, and the time to do it is before the interviewing process. Having a job offer in hand is tempting, but it is not right if it heads you in a direction that will not fulfill your personal goals. Some jobs present a glamorous image and offer better-than-average starting salaries, but they also may turn out to be dead ends. Other jobs, though perceived as ordinary and slow starting, may offer some excellent long-term benefits.

When trying to land that first job, there may not be much choice due to financial circumstances, but try to avoid a hasty decision if at all possible. It is prudent to be deliberate in taking this first step. Your future is your responsibility alone; no one else can or should make those decisions for you.

It is advantageous to take some time to investigate a range of career options. There are many choices, from fast food to fine dining and the often-overlooked institutional food service market. The opportunity to rise to the highest levels in any of these sectors is equally open to those who have knowledge, skill, and ambition. Seniors at either four- or two-year food service schools are prime candidates for many starting positions presented by eager recruiters. However, those without a formal education but with experience are also in heavy demand.

Pursuing the best employer for you is one of the most important decisions of your career. If knowledge is power and experience is in demand, then what you should most want from your first employer is a good professional training program. The training should place great emphasis on the fundamentals of good food service at the ground-floor level. It is within this early period of a career that the time to sharpen your skills in the basic details of food production and service is available. Later on there will not be many opportunities, and time will be limited because of growing management responsibilities. Take advantage of the training offered early in your career because it will offer you that extra edge to compete successfully over time.

While searching for a first job it is imperative to investigate all prospective employers' commitments to providing training for their new management hires. Beware of casual remarks concerning this aspect of long-term professional development. Though they will not admit it, some companies will readily cut back expenditures in this area when profits begin to fall. It is a short-term outlook, but unfortunately it often occurs when management is under pressure to meet the company's monthly and quarterly profit goals.

If your first job choice does not turn out as well as expected, you need not worry that your dream career is over. Sometimes you have to chalk it up to experience and learn from it. From tough times valuable lessons can be learned, and it's good to find out early what you like and what you don't like. This will provide you with a basis from which to make better decisions in the future. Constantly changing jobs should be avoided, but if something doesn't feel right, keep on searching for better opportunities and do not be afraid to move on.

There has been much consolidation of companies in recent years, so many choices will be with larger organizations. Do not be reluctant to start with a large company. It can have a great deal of resources and much to offer. Many people imagine that they will have to put up with a great deal of bureaucracy in a large, impersonal company. They may be fearful they will not be treated as individuals but considered simply as a number. This is not necessarily true, but by doing some investigation ahead of time, you can find out. Try to talk with some people who are currently employed with the company or have been in the past. Ask questions about the company's philosophy of doing business, training programs, opportunities for advancement, and reward systems. When going through the interview process, ask to visit one of its facilities to see its operations firsthand and to have an opportunity to meet with some of its personnel. Being denied such a request is unlikely, and your sincere inquiry will certainly make a positive impression on the interviewer. Good companies are proud of their operations and their people and are always eager to impress top candidates. This is a major reason for their success and could be what makes a large organization the best choice for a first job.

You may prefer working for a small, independent company. Working for an individual operator may be fine, but be sure it is a person who will take an objective interest and concern with your development. If the potential employer is a relative or a friend, be cautious. Be sure that it is not simply mutual convenience. It is your future here that is most at stake, not ease of employment.

Questions need to be asked and the ramifications evaluated with a clear mind. Evaluate just how knowledgeable and experienced a prospective employer is, such as whether the manager readily admits not knowing it all or profoundly claims to be able to teach you everything you need to know about the business; the latter should be a warning sign. A real professional will readily acknowledge he or she still has a lot to learn and will always try to keep learning. Many have attested to this fact. This does not mean the individual does not have exceptional knowledge, but know he or she may have only a one-sided opinion on a number of subjects based primarily on personal experience. That is good to a degree, but times change and so do the intricacies of the food service business. You need not shy away from a valuable opportunity, but understand the limitations.

On the other hand, when working in a large organization, there is a chance for exposure to more various points of view due to the diversity of the individuals. An expert in food may not be an expert in accounting or customer service. All these skills require a depth of knowledge and experience that one person may not be able to master entirely. On balance, there is greater depth and more opportunity to learn from a diverse group as opposed to an individual employer. This can be a distinct advantage for the new manager on his or her first job, when the objective should be to learn as much as possible.

For those who feel they would eventually enjoy the smaller or single operation, I would recommend first to start out with the larger firm that has more to offer as far as initial training is concerned. After a year or two you can change your mind, but if not, you can bring that much more knowledge and practical experience to the next job. An independent employer will appreciate and value your services even more, which means they might be willing to start a new employee off with a higher salary. Having earned it by paying your dues, you shouldn't hesitate to negotiate from strength.

If you do decide to make a change, do not feel guilty about leaving the larger firm. You may have received valuable training and experience, but you also worked hard and contributed to the organization. Both parties have profited. Besides, if the organization wants to keep an employee, it will find a way to provide him or her with the opportunities and monetary incentives to remain. At least, smart bosses will find a way, as they are the ones who believe in finding and growing the best talent for their organization. They know that they are only as good as their subordinates make them. What remains for you is to keep an open mind and to decide which road offers you the best opportunity for the future.

The quality of management training is one aspect to investigate, but the training that is provided by a prospective employer for the hourly employees is just as important. Often, you will hear the saying, "We are only as good as our people." These are great words to live by, but unfortunately, the words often carry only the intention, and once again the tight budget arises. The training of hourly workers requires a larger commitment from a broader section of management at a higher cost. These should not be sacrificed for the benefit of a few select management programs the company decides are easier and less expensive to provide.

Neglecting the frontline employees is foolhardy. These are the people who prepare and serve the food and who ultimately have the most direct customer contact. A company that neglects this responsibility will, in the long run, pay a high price. The practical result of little or no training is quite evident in any food service establishment. The facility is not clean or neat, service is not friendly, and food quality is inconsistent, eventually sending the establishment out of business. It results in disappointment for the customer, the management, and the owner. This obviously is not the place for a management trainee to start a career.

It has been noted that employees who are provided with training recognize the interest that the company places in them. The usual result is that not only is the job done well, but also the employees are happier and satisfied with their employer. The result is less turnover and lower costs, not to mention satisfied customers who not only return more frequently, but also tell their friends. When the time comes when someone in your organization says it cannot afford the training budget for this current tough period, tell that person emphatically that it doesn't make good business sense to discontinue the program. There may be more resistance than one might expect, but it is worth the battle to stand firm. Good training does not necessarily cost a lot of money. It is more a matter of management taking the time and making the effort. In many cases, it simply boils down to good communication on a daily basis.

The most productive operations that I have observed take the time to meet daily with their employees to discuss matters relative to production, service, housekeeping, client relations, safety, or other pertinent information of the day. Employees like to be informed, and management's willingness to openly share information is a sign of respect. Smart managers hold their employees in high regard and as valuable assets to the business. Accordingly, employees who sense they are appreciated are inclined to work more cooperatively as a team when they are armed with information and have an understanding of everyone's role. Formality does not make much difference; consistency is more important. This style of management sends the message that employees are important and are to be treated as responsible individuals with a contribution to make. It creates a working atmosphere that is indisputably positive for fulfilling the purposes of the business and is what forward-looking management should be all about. Therefore, taking the time to investigate the style of management practiced in a company is an important factor when considering employment with an organization.

Once you are a new manager on the company payroll, you will begin training and development toward a bright future, but remember there is never an end to it. An employer may get you started, but it is up to you to apply yourself. There are many opportunities, but taking advantage of them will be strictly up to you. Company libraries are filled with operating manuals that will not be a benefit to anyone unless they are used. Self-discipline and study will be rewarded. If you want to get by with just minimum effort, future prospects will be limited. If in the past you have ignored the appeals of parents and teachers to work with earnest, then it may be a difficult change. Now is the time to get with the program!

Do not underestimate the complexity of the food service industry. Being a part of it is not an easy occupation. Changes happen rapidly, and standards are constantly being raised. Customers are constantly expecting more. Thus, learning is a continuous process. The managers who grow into higher levels of success understand that and assume the responsibility for their own self-development. They do not wait to be helped by their supervisors or the human resources department. Those who are successful take the initiative to seek out every possible training opportunity. They read industry publications and participate in professional organizations where they become more knowledgeable. It is a mind-set for those who want to succeed and who have the desire. It is solely up to you how far you want to go. The more effort you are willing to put into your profession, the more you will get out of it. It is not always how smart you are, but how hard you are willing to work.

Making a career decision is difficult enough, and it is only the beginning. Soon it is time to interact with the real world, where the options become more complex and the decisions are even tougher to make. As you pursue interviews with prospective employers, and I recommend the more the merrier, you should look for opportunities to get a feel for what working at a particular organization would be like. Sometimes the glamour or the imagined prestige of certain jobs is appealing, which can have a strong influence on your decision. Also the skill and the attractiveness of the interviewer can sway you into a field that may not be in your best interest. This is not the time to decide emotionally but rather with the utmost care. It is the time for thoughtful insight and to carefully measure the opportunity against the personal goals you have already put into writing. This does not mean you cannot be flexible in your thinking and make some adjustments where necessary. But it is important to keep an open mind and to carefully weigh the alternatives. Just do not feel compelled to decide abruptly or be pressured into making any rapid U-turns from seeking your personal goal.

Without a well-conceived personal plan, some individuals seem to get started in a field purely by accident. It just happened to be available when a job was needed, or it was the best or the only opportunity at the time. Some people are persuaded because they have a friend working for a prospective employer who seems to be well satisfied. These are the wrong reasons to jump at the first offer. That first job is critical, for it sets you in a direction that may not be easy to change later when circumstances and obligations might make it prohibitive. It is not easy to take the time to make a thoughtful decision when the pressure is on to get employed. The key is to remain focused on the kind of the life ahead of you that you want so that you will be motivated to do some serious investigation.

A good first step is to ask some tough questions about what working in the business world is all about. Are you prepared and willing to make the sacrifices needed to succeed? In most service industries, particularly the food service industry, there will be heavy demands on your time. You will find that when many of your friends are playing, you will be on the job. It just comes with the territory.

Give some thought to the following questions. Your answers may help you determine if you want to pursue a career in food service management:

1. Do I have the drive and ambition to make the personal sacrifices necessary to achieve a high degree of success?

2. Am I willing to work the extra hours necessary to manage large responsibilities? Do I mind giving up weekends and evenings if the job requires this kind of schedule?

3. Do I enjoy the subject of food and beverages, and would I explore and continue to study the many areas of this subject freely on my own time? Is it a chore or a real interest?

4. Am I a well-organized person who understands the importance of the details that make a business tick? Am I profit motivated? Do I realize that no matter how much I enjoy the work, the business still has to make a return on investment?

5. Am I a service-oriented person who believes in the status and professionalism of the work, or do I feel inferior because I am always providing service to others?

6. Can I be enthusiastic about the business and set an example for employees and coworkers? Can I cope with adversity with an optimistic spirit and deal effectively with the everyday problems of running a business?

7. Do I appreciate the value of all people, especially the ones who will be my employees? Do I have a common respect and appreciation for the value of the work required at all levels of the food service operation?

Granted, there are numerous other self-evaluations to make before you leap into the food service business, and they should be explored as thoroughly as possible. Talk to people in the various fields, ask them what it takes to be successful, and ask about the life style that goes along with it.

For believers in aptitude and personality tests, there are a number of ways to learn more about yourself. Universities, schools, career counselors, or a personal psychologist are all good sources for aptitude testing that can increase your awareness of the areas that are of most interest to you. A worthwhile exercise to learn more about yourself can help you make a more informed career decision.

Test results may not define the exact work you are suited for, but they will point toward areas where you will have the best chance for success. Of course, your test results may show that you are so well-rounded you will succeed in any career. That is wonderful; being a well-rounded person is a good thing, especially for someone interested in a food management career. It is the type of work where having a sense of balance and a variety of skills is important. You must have the inclination and the ability to deal with a wide variety of people and circumstances. Each day is different, and the challenges will test the best in you. Now is the time to think about what you want out of life. Deciding is not always easy. Sometimes it comes down to listening to what your gut tells you, and then just doing it!

Chapter 2

Deciding on Your Options

(Life can be normal, well… almost.)

As you pursue interviews with prospective employers, you should try to get a feel for what working in a particular field would be like. Do not trust your imagination, for it may lead to disappointment when reality sets in. You cannot get a good picture of a prospective employer if the interview takes place in a fancy hotel room. Make a concerted effort to visit an operation or two where food production and service can be seen firsthand. Talk to the food service managers on the job and some of the employees, too. Take the full tour and ask questions. From on-site investigation, you can get a better idea of how the company operates and how it treats its personnel. It tells the real story, and your efforts will be worthwhile in helping you come to the right decision. A good company will welcome your interest and make these opportunities available.

If the field of food service seems exciting but the idea of working nights and weekends is not appealing, take heart, for there are many other viable career options besides public service restaurants. Though perhaps not as glamorous and certainly not as widely publicized, there are many exceptional opportunities in the institutional market. At the same time these careers offer life styles that many refer to as "normal." That means if mostly days, minimal weekend requirements, and traditional holiday time for family activities is what you have in mind, the institutional market offers some desirable advantages. There are a wide variety of opportunities. Considering the following may help narrow the field.

Healthcare: This market is rapidly growing and has tremendous opportunities for qualified dietary food service managers. Healthcare includes hospitals, retirement homes, and skilled nursing homes that pay quite well to those who can effectively operate their food service departments. There are holiday and weekend work requirements, as healthcare operations do run 365 days a year. Because of these circumstances, most healthcare food service departments insist on adequate supervisory staffing to provide the necessary coverage. Of course, the newly hired assistant food service manager is usually assigned the least desirable schedule, but even that is not necessarily bad. Most administrators are wise enough to know that in situations requiring extensive service coverage, work assignments must be fair if they are going to keep good employees.

As you progress up the ladder to the top food service position, the working hours may coincide more with a normal business schedule. However, the one in charge is still responsible for all that happens in the department. Though the top position deserves the most favorable schedule, the responsible leader will always voluntarily look in periodically on the operation during weekends and holiday periods to inspect the quality of service. In reality, one of the reasons someone acquires a promotion is because he or she has a sense of responsibility. It is one of the most important characteristics of an effective leader, and those who demonstrate it willingly are recognized by the healthcare administrators — and they of course are the ones making the decisions on whom to promote.

For those who are interested in the field of healthcare food service management, the following list includes some basic requirements:

1. The ability to work at a high professional level and to be able to communicate effectively with the administrative staff, dietitians, and to some degree with doctors and nurses.

2. Must be well organized and highly competent in administration since the healthcare field requires expert record-keeping and documentation. You will also be required to cooperate and respond to frequent inspections by the state and other certification agencies.

3. Have a high regard for the value of dietetics and its importance in patient health maintenance and recovery.

4. Have high personal standards and extraordinary diligence when it comes to departmental cleanliness and sanitation.

5. Have the skill to train employees in various food service subjects because their skills must be more exact when it comes to preparing and serving special diets to patients under strict medical care.

6. Keeping current with the latest healthcare food service practices is a must, and continuing to update professional credentials is extremely important. Many opportunities are available for continuous education provided by national and state associations.

Healthcare food service is not just about food trays and bland recipes for the sick. Culinary expertise and creativity play a major role in providing special meals for recovering patients and their families. The demands and expectations of the staff cafeteria, the coffee shop, and the private dining rooms require the expertise of a well-rounded, professional food service manager. Holiday promotions of all kinds and creating other sources of departmental income through inside and outside catering is an important part of controlling the department's budget. Going beyond the minimum of patient service requirements is critical for those who expect to succeed. Healthcare is not a one-dimensional arena, so never think it is only a dull routine. It can be as exciting and glamorous as you make it.

For those who qualify, healthcare is a challenging and rewarding career within the food service management field and should be considered seriously by those who aspire to a more customary life style. This is a good choice where you can arrange time for a reasonable personal life and still fully serve the demands of your career.

Colleges and Universities: If an academic atmosphere and interacting with mostly young people is enticing, this field of food service management is an interesting prospect. Other aspects include serving the faculty, staff, and the revered athletic department. There is a variety of clientele, all concentrated in a miniature city, which makes for an interesting challenge. There are more institutions in this field than are realized: huge or small, in large cities or remote areas, and everything in between. There are private colleges, public colleges, religious colleges, and community colleges, all serving people who believe education will better their lives. All those people require meals, and the field is still growing to meet an ever-increasing demand.

For those who remember less-than-exciting college or school cafeterias and imagine the job of food service director to be monotonous, dull, and unappreciated, think again. Times have changed dramatically, and many campuses today provide a wide variety of unique and popular food service programs. In addition, the delivery of first-class catering services is a basic requirement expected from the food service department. Catering can run the gamut, from outdoor barbecues to continental cuisine, and surprisingly, it is the major source of revenue for the food service department. The service can be as stylish as the finest hotel downtown or as casual as a church picnic, all depending on the talent, skills, and imagination of the food service staff.

In response to this demand, campus administrators have increased their efforts to recruit and select only the most talented and experienced food service directors. Salary scales have also risen accordingly.

Though on most campuses the cafeteria still provides students with their basic nutritional needs, you will also find several additional food service stations offering a variety of choices. Some of the options available are grill stations serving premium burgers, chicken sandwiches, and steak sandwiches, along with a choice of different styles of fries and accompaniments; wok stations serving oriental food to order; pasta stations featuring a choice of sauces prepared with fresh herbs; and deli stations making sandwiches to order. Add to that dessert stations, beverage stations, and carry out, and it is comparable to a small mall right on campus. It no longer compares with yesterday's institutional food services.

Colleges and universities have been progressive in recent years marketing to the student body the kinds of food students have grown up eating. The proliferation of fast food and the impact of advertising have had a major influence on the taste and food preferences of today's college generation. Since many grew up wandering through the spreading suburban malls, they have developed an affinity for the popular fast food denizens, such as Burger King, Chick-fil-A, Taco Bell, Subway, McDonald's, Pizza Hut, Dunkin' Donuts, and popular local eateries. Many of these brand name companies have put together franchise contracts with the higher educational institutions. They have found that increased student satisfaction and the resulting higher sales income has more than compensated for the added facility investment and the franchise fees.

A manager on a major campus today will most likely have the responsibility for operating any one or several of these brand name food services. In many ways this has been an attractive arrangement for both parties. The company offers ongoing training, quality control inspections, and marketing support to build interest and improve sales. The college generates more income because of the name recognition and the popularity of the company's menu, and costs are lower because the system has proven to operate at a high degree of efficiency. The brand name company also benefits by having another franchisee, which further builds its reputation and produces additional franchise fees. The college and university food service field is a wide and diverse one. If this is an arena where you would enjoy working, consider some of the following requirements.

A college food service director must have a spirited attitude about the institution and toward the entire student body, faculty, and administration. Having a sense of family, loyalty to the school, and a respect for tradition is important on a college campus.

It is important to become acquainted with campus student leaders and to keep abreast of campus issues. Do not worry if food services at times becomes an issue for debate. It comes with the territory so be prepared for it. Being defensive, whether right or wrong, is a recipe for disaster. Take it in, admit mistakes, and affirm to make improvements. Honest humility will carry the day, you will earn respect, and offenses will be forgiven.

Demonstrations are often a rite of passage for students who need to let off steam and relieve some frustration from their studies. Other than the issue of campus parking, food service is a tempting target for an insurgence. The best strategy to minimize damage is to have a positive relationship with the current student party in power. Yes, it's good old politics, but it helps smooth out the rough road a manager will certainly be traveling.

Campus newspapers are notorious for cutting their investigative and cynical teeth on the food service department. It is an everyday personal issue, and to some degree it keeps the students' attention off the administration. The students' perception of the current semester's food services is their reality. Last semester's performance is history. That is why political connections are best kept up to date, because those student leaders in power change every year. Students are not overly complimentary about their campus food service program no matter how good the staff thinks it is, so this is not the kind of work for those with tender egos. Being defensive just exacerbates the situation so if your skin is thin it is better not to venture into the mine-laden field of campus dining. The food service director's position demands humility, patience, and a willingness to listen, and as long as an attempt is made to respond to their concerns, whether real or not, a manager will come to realize the students do not want to cause harm. They are consumers just like anybody else. They pay their money, and they do not want to be taken advantage of because they are to some degree a captured audience. They want better, and they deserve it.

School Lunch: If school lunch does not bring back fond images of culinary delights and a variety of choices, then you may not have attended a school lunch program lately. The advancement of many school lunch programs may be surprising. Though not as sophisticated as some of the advances in higher educational food services, there have been considerable improvements. Grills serving fresh burgers, hot pizza straight from the oven, and salad bars have found their way into many of today's school lunch programs. There are still numerous stereotypical "lunch-ladies" faithfully providing nutritious meals for today's children. And, when it comes to good housekeeping you will not find kitchens kept cleaner anywhere. Lunch ladies continue to be the backbone of the school lunch program, and the job would be impossible without their sense of loyalty and sincere caring for each schoolchild. We should be proud and supportive of the women who have given faithful service over many years.

School lunch today is a big business that requires an expert hand to manage a significant part of the school budget. It is not just about preparing lunches five days a week. Good public relations, political acumen, and communication skills are essential, as the lunch management is required to answer to the local school board and concerned neighborhood taxpayers. Think about being responsible for producing and serving several thousand lunches a day, which is the case in many of our major cities. That is a monumental logistic and management challenge that will test the best and brightest members of the food service profession.

Business and Industry: There was a time when many companies provided free or reduced-price meals for their employees. It was one of the fringe benefits, along with several others, such as paid insurance premiums, that kept employees, though relatively low paid, loyal to their employers. Most of these paternalistic practices have been discontinued during recent years due to pressures from employees and unions for better paychecks. Inexpensive lunches were not perceived as significant compared to better hourly pay rates, and therefore companies saw this as an opportunity to reduce overhead expenses. It became impractical, especially for companies who had reduced their employment to the point where the company cafeteria did not even have enough traffic to sustain sufficient revenue, and the investment required to modernize the food service facilities became out of the question. Also, the development of nearby fast food establishments became more appealing to employees than mundane cafeteria food, further reducing employee participation.

Many company cafeterias were converted to "break rooms," and vending services became the style of service. This is a part of the era of a nutritional nightmare, but cost-cutting and freedom of choice were forces of progress not to ignore. So where is the opportunity today for what appears to be a dying industry? They may be few, but those company food services that have survived have done so by modernizing and by improving their quality and service to meet today's consumer demand. Look for the major companies, especially at their headquarter locations, where there are often exquisite facilities and well-run operations. They are staffed with professional managers, and some include highly skilled chefs.

Many business and industry food services are under contract to food service management companies, but there are still a good number who insist on running their own. Starting a career with one of the independent operations will not likely lead to rapid advancement, because most company-operated food services simply do not have the resources or time to train and develop people from the ground up. If this is a field in which you are interested, begin working for a good food service management company. Once you have the experience and a strong résumé, you can then become a candidate for all kinds of other opportunities.

During the early stages of working for a management company, there may be a number of job transfers, as companies require mobility to staff new openings. Therefore, they seek out candidates for advancement first from those who are willing to pull up stakes and move, and for young and ambitious people with few strings attached, now is the time to take risks and be ready to make changes. To be enthusiastic and responsive to company needs is a real plus for getting ahead, and building a reputation for company loyalty will be in your favor to collect those bigger rewards and promotions in the future. The better opportunities are more likely to become available to those who are willing to pay their dues.

A top management position running food service for a large industrial company is something to be coveted. The working conditions are extraordinary, since service hours are limited to breakfast and lunch, Monday through Friday. There may be a few special banquets during evenings or on weekends, but compared to most other working conditions in the food service industry, it is a piece of cake. The environment is normally first class, and support from the company's maintenance and housekeeping departments in most cases keeps equipment and facilities in top condition. The best positions are few, so to get one in this business and industry market, prepare well and be ready for some tough competition.

Restaurant Chains: Both national and regional restaurant chains have considerable employment action, for this is where restaurant companies are most desperately in need of new talent. Their employment ads dominate the help wanted sections in newspapers. It is relatively easy to get a starting job in this market, but investigate carefully before making the plunge. Remember the importance of that first job. Be certain if a career in restaurants is where you want to be in the future. To attain lofty goals in the restaurant industry and develop a well-rounded knowledge of food service, be particular. You should try to interview with those who appear to have the depth of menu and sophistication that will challenge your ambition. Find out about the type of training they offer and the opportunity for getting hands-on experience. A few classes on how to refer to the company manuals is not professional development. Ask about the technical people a company employs, such as chefs, dietitians, analysts, and particularly trainers. Put starting salary aside at the beginning, and concentrate on the quality of the training and the experience available. The right kind of groundwork at this stage can make a big difference down the road.

A start with the major chains can be one of the best ways to begin a career. The hours are long and the work is demanding, but this is the perfect place for someone young and full of energy and burning ambition. It is fast paced, it is highly social, it is fun, and it is where the "bright lights" are.

Independent Restaurants: Unless it is part of a family-run business, an independent restaurant may be the least favorable place to start a food service career. If it is solely a seasonal job or part-time while going through school, it may be a good way to get a feel for the business and to determine if it is a desirable life style. If it is a successfully well-run operation, it will be a good example. However, when it comes to building a successful career, one depends on the ability of the owner-operator who is willing and able to provide a learning experience based on sound operating principals. Unfortunately, this type of ideal situation is the exception rather than the rule. In the real world, there are more poorly run and mediocre operations than there are good ones. It is the primary reason why the failure rate is so high for restaurants. There are many success stories, but that does not necessarily mean they are well managed.

It is easy to become overly impressed by the apparent success of a particular business and assume management must be doing something right, though the success may be due to other factors: a great location, a captured audience, or a lack of current competition. It might be successful in spite of itself. The things to look for are examples of good management, sound fundamentals, and the level of customer satisfaction. Of course, those new at this may have difficulty determining that, but if you have any common sense you should be able to fathom whether the owner-operator you are working for knows his or her stuff and acts professionally. Consider whether it is a type of management style you consider worth emulating. Then again, sometimes much can be learned from the actions and mistakes of a poor manager. Bad examples can provide some valuable lessons about how not to do things, and sooner or later everyone encounters a bad experience. You tend to remember them the best, and at least they're a good resource for your personal war stories.

Working in a family restaurant that is part of your own family can be appealing, but there are shortcomings. An important element to be concerned about is the risk of not becoming your own person. The senior member in charge usually maintains a firm control over the business and is likely to retain power for making the major decisions because it may be difficult for him or her to delegate real responsibility. Family owners can be too strict or too easygoing when it comes to supervising close relatives, and when the principals are emotionally involved, management development is easily compromised. There is a tendency, though not intentional, to protect the family from difficult and demanding situations. Sometimes it is just the opposite, where the son or daughter is given responsibility before he or she is ready. It is a difficult job in which to stay objective and to deal fairly with relatives and at the same time with the other non-relatives who also are part of the work force. That does not mean it cannot be done, but these potential drawbacks are something for the new career person, and the elders who are in charge, to think about. Besides, nothing is more irksome for employees than having to work under an inexperienced and presumptuous son or daughter of the owner. However, if parents are smart and have the willingness to challenge as well as train their child properly like a true professional, the young man or woman is indeed fortunate.

Food Service Management Companies: The demand for management personnel by food service management companies is one of the most extensive in the industry. You can find their recruiting ads in major newspapers and in most trade magazines. For the past few decades, more institutions have been calling on professional management companies to operate their food service departments. There are several practical reasons, but the most pressing is the difficulty for an independently run institution to retain a highly qualified food service director for a long time. Operating a food service department successfully has become more complex, especially since today's consumer has higher expectations than ever and has considerably more choices. Cost containment is also a major factor, so it takes an exceptional individual to balance quality service while minimizing operating expenses.

Management companies have been effective in fulfilling those needs and concerns. They have the capability to provide their clients with a qualified on-site food service manager, and they can back up that person with an experienced professional food service supervisor. This combination of talent takes a considerable burden off the client, while assuring a well-run food service program. Add a host of experts, from seasoned chefs to legal advisors, and include guarantees concerning adherence to the budget, and there exists an offer that is hard to refuse.

The companies today are advanced and extremely sophisticated in marketing and are willing to make commitments regarding major investments for upgrading antiquated facilities when necessary. It is a highly competitive industry where the major participants have earned excellent reputations for delivering quality performance and for their cost-containing results. They are tenacious, dedicated to their clients, and extremely responsive to correcting problems. Their dedication to "exceed expectations" and their attentiveness to their clients' demands have achieved great results by retaining some of their service contracts for more than 30 years.

A career with a first-class company can be rewarding monetarily and offers unlimited opportunity for professional growth. Interview with several of the best, and be sure to ask direct questions about the type and breadth of the management training and career development you can expect. If you are willing to invest time and energy to perform at the best level, you should expect the same kind of investment from the company. However, you must be aware that you will have to be ready to pack up and move to the company location where you are most needed. Being too particular about where or under what specific conditions you prefer to work will just limit opportunity. However, being willing to cooperate for the good of the company may lead toward a successful career and a great adventure.

Unless you are in a hurry to get that first paycheck, be prepared to do some real searching, and interview as often as possible. It is not a life-or-death decision, but remember: Once settled into a job, there is a tendency to get so absorbed in the daily routine that it can be difficult to make a change later.

Recognize that any experience obtained early in a career, no matter how devastating, can still provide valuable lessons. Some of your worst encounters will give you insight into certain areas you don't want to pursue. Finally, keep your written long-term goals close, and stick fast to your dreams. Often the path to your objective is not a straight line, which may be for the ultimate good, since the bumps encountered along the way will broaden your knowledge and help strengthen your determination. Overcoming and dealing well with those early difficulties will make your eventual success and achievements in the field of food service that much better.

Chapter 3

Predicting Your Food Cost

Everyone who goes into business, whether it is a large or small enterprise, starts with a dream. It begins with a creative idea concerning a product or a service that you see growing into a grand success. You are excited and cannot wait to start the day because it is what you love to do. A dream builds confidence and expectations of customers who will come clamoring to buy your goods or services. Yes, this dream sounds sweet, but do not forget the real purpose of going into business and being successful: it is about making money. It is about the bottom line, the profitability, and understanding all the pertinent numbers that go into making up that bottom line. Profits are essential to pay the suppliers, the employees, the banker, and, most of all, those fidgety investors. A business cannot grow successfully unless there is a profit, and that requires management staying on top of the numbers and knowing what the numbers mean. Making money off a dream is great, but if it does not make a profit, you will not be doing so for long.

The food management business may be more perplexing than most when it comes to getting a handle on the numbers, as there are so many of them. It becomes even more difficult to predict with great precision because the chief product, prepared food, is always in a continuous perishable state. Though troublesome, it is still important to be able to predict with some reliability the cost of goods sold, the highest category of business expense. To this end, the most critical part is knowing the exact cost of every item on the menu and understanding how these numbers influence profitability. For example, if you know that in order for your food service operation to be profitable you must achieve a 35 percent food cost, then it is essential to construct a menu that will produce that objective. To do so, someone has to do the work of pre-costing every recipe and every product that is included in the menu. It is amazing how many food service operators bypass this important first step. The industry has a bad reputation for just winging it, and it may be because some feel food service is solely an art, not a science. In reality it is a little of both.

Many food service managers and even restaurant owners do not bother to go through the task of pre-costing their menu, which is primarily a cost analysis of every recipe. The reason is simply that it requires too much tedious detail work. Not only is this a poor excuse, but also many newcomers to the business do not know how to go about it. Because of the extra effort required, it is often avoided, and unfortunately, the pre-costing process becomes secondary to all the other time-consuming obstacles that must be overcome when starting a new business. Besides, many food service operators think they should be able to make a quick estimate from experience to predetermine the cost of the menu. Making shortcut estimates, however, has historically driven many food service enterprises unknowingly out of business.

Someone once advised me to think of the pre-costing process as though I was determining the cost of manufacturing a car or a TV set. GM, Ford, and Sony do not build cars or DVDs and sell them without knowing exactly what the materials cost. However, few food service operators, particularly the independents, do an exact pre-costing of their recipes and menus before they commence service. It is assumed that when problems start, changes can be made along the way. That is fine, but many do not know where to look, and frequent arbitrary changes can disrupt a business that is trying to get off the ground.

Let us review the planning process. It begins by understanding the basic formula for establishing prices when the cost is known. If maintaining a 35 percent food cost for profitability is required, calculate the selling price by dividing each recipe's total cost, including all the accompaniments, by 35, and the result will be the selling price. However, it is not as easy as that because there are many other factors that affect your true food cost that have to be taken into consideration. Prices need to be set realistically and at a level that is acceptable in the marketplace. Therefore, it is imperative to arrive at your menu prices by starting with an analysis of the market beforehand. The sensible owner or manager will set the prices in his local area at the level that will attract the maximum number of potential customers, while still producing top profitability. This will mean checking the prices of the competition and analyzing what the customers in your market are willing to pay. Successful businesses spend a great deal of time engaged in these studies to decide on their best course of action before opening their doors.

At this point, a range of menu prices that fall within the customer's limits of acceptability should be established. Now is the time to refine those prices so the highest level of gross profit can be achieved. Once the ideal food cost percentage essential for maximum profits is determined, remember to take into consideration the other elements that will certainly add to that cost. It is more than just pre-costing recipes. The cost of additional staples must be included. These may include seasonings, condiments, cooking oils, breads, or any other items that make up the food service program. An alternate method is to factor 2 to 3 percent additional cost into each recipe to come up with a total recipe cost as a basis to determine selling prices. How much will depend on the extent of the service. Nothing comes for free. These items, if overlooked, can considerably cut into profitability.

Do not expect food preparation to work out perfectly every time. There will undoubtedly be some production errors and a certain amount of waste. Take into consideration the cost of employee meals, discounts, and promotions. These variables also have to be factored into the cost of food consumed to calculate adequate selling prices. Therefore, to attain an overall 35 percent food cost, recipes in total must come to something less. This is a difficult one to calculate exactly and will depend to a great extent on the complexity and the breadth of the menu, total sales volume, and the skills of the employees. Limited fast food menus obviously need a minimum addition, whereby a continental cuisine menu made up of unusual and seasonal ingredients may need a considerably higher addition. You will have to analyze the specifics of your program carefully and use good judgment. Say, for example, that variables should amount to 2 percent of total gross sales. Therefore, for a 35 percent food cost, be sure that the total average recipe cost is no more than 33 percent. If an operation is managed properly and costs are controlled, you should be able to maintain the 35 percent food cost that the profit requires. Be prepared, though, to experience higher food costs at the beginning of any new food service operation. There will be a learning curve for everyone, including management. The level of completeness and preparedness of preliminary plans will determine how quickly top productivity and targeted profits are reached.

Let us say that 12 key items on the menu have been determined through research to require selling prices from $5.95 to $12.50. With that knowledge, proceed to pre-cost the menu by analyzing the ingredients of each menu recipe. If a salad or a vegetable is included in a main menu item, do not forget to include that cost when calculating the total food cost percentage for that particular item. By using your computer, it should be easy to set up a simple spreadsheet program, such as Excel, for the task. This will save a great deal of time, and the results are mathematically accurate. When conditions change, the program is already set up for quick and easy adjustments. If you are not comfortable with computers, hire a part-time person who is familiar with the spreadsheet program, and tell that person what needs to be accomplished. Chances are good that you can find a member of the wait staff who is quite competent and will be overjoyed to be asked to provide some high-tech assistance. Also, you should be able to locate a pre-developed recipe pre-costing program that will suit your needs and accomplish the job with quick efficiency. Extraordinary programming and expensive technical assistance are not required, only a simple program with mathematical capabilities.

First, a detailed recipe for each item on the menu needs to be enumerated. A competent chef should be capable of providing that information. You need not be discouraged if you have employed a chef who insists on keeping his or her "secret recipes" all locked up in his or her head. It may be easier to crack open a coconut, but an owner or manager should have some leverage if he or she is writing the paychecks. Take a deep breath, decide who is in charge, and be determined to obtain this critical information. First, know the portion size of the main ingredient and the measurements of all the other recipe components that make up the final product. The recipe is essential for producing a tasty dish and for standardizing the cost of the product. Consistency is the key to success in the food business for the benefit of the customer and the operator. Irregular portions not only destroy control, but are also upsetting to customers. Management must first establish the correct portion size for every item on the menu and train the production staff so that everyone understands the importance of exact portioning. Being strict and having high standards are management responsibilities that cannot be relinquished. Leaving the future of your business to chance is unacceptable.

Ingredients cannot be measured to the tenth of an ounce, but they can be within an acceptable range. Give a little allowance for small errors, but be diligent and use common sense. Try to include in the analysis everything offered with the menu item at that specific selling price. In the two following illustrations, vegetables and bread were identified and pre-costed. Do this also if a soup or salad is offered; this will help prevent anything from being overlooked. Sometimes the little things that slip by cost the most.

After the program is set up, recipe cost changes can be calculated quickly by posting in the purchasing cost changes for any ingredient. The purchase prices in the recipe examples that follow are averages that before long will be out of date. Ingredient price changes must be recorded periodically, or the information on recipe costs will be wrong. (Note: Though your spreadsheet will provide you with a total cost of the menu item ingredients, you must still first set your selling price in a range that will be acceptable to your potential customers noted as "Market Acceptability." Then your food cost percentage is a result of the total cost divided by your predetermined acceptable price.)

RECIPE COST ANALYSIS — FILLET MIGNON WITH MUSTARD CREAM SAUCE				
Ingredients	Portion/oz/ each	Purchase Cost/lb.	Cost per oz.	Portion Cost
Filet Mignon	8	$10.50	$0.66	$5.28
Butter	1	$1.95	$0.12	$0.12
Vegetable Oil	0.5	$1.15	$0.07	$0.04
Salt & Pepper				$0.03
Shallot	2	$1.60	$0.10	$0.20
Brandy	1	$6.00	$0.38	$0.38
Whipping Cream	2.5	$2.10	$0.13	$0.33
Dijon	0.5	$2.40	$0.15	$0.08
Fresh Parsley				$0.04
Total Entrée Cost				**$6.50**
Accompaniments				

RECIPE COST ANALYSIS — FILLET MIGNON WITH MUSTARD CREAM SAUCE				
Ingredients	Portion/oz/ each	Purchase Cost/lb.	Cost per oz.	Portion Cost
Potatoes				$0.25
Asparagus				$0.65
Bread & Butter				$0.50
Total Cost				$7.90
Food Cost %				39.00%
Selling Price				$20.25
Market Acceptability				

RECIPE COST ANALYSIS — CHICKEN ITALIANO				
Ingredients	Portion/oz/ each	Purchase Cost/lb.	Cost per oz.	Portion Cost
Chicken Breast	10	$2.49	$0.16	$1.60
Olive Oil	1	$4.35	$0.27	$0.27
Fresh Tomato	2	$2.65	$0.17	$0.34
Fresh Garlic	0.5	$3.90	$0.24	$0.12
Fresh Basil	0.5		$0.35	$0.18
Total Entrée Cost				$2.51
Accompaniments				
Fettuccini	2	$1.40	$0.09	$0.18
Bread & Butter				$0.50
Total Cost				$3.19
Food Cost %				20%
Selling Price				$15.95
Market Acceptability				$0.65

Pre-costing each recipe is only the first step since the ultimate food cost will depend primarily on the menu mix of sales. To do this, project how many of each menu item you expect to sell. Someone with restaurant sales experience should be able to help in projecting some realistic numbers. The following illustration attempts to determine what the ideal food cost might be in the category of entrees when a sales mix of entrees is projected.

Menu Item	Selling Price	Pre- Cost	Cost %	Projected Unit Sale	$ Sale # Units X Price	$ Cost # Units X Cost
Filet Mignon	$20.25	$7.90	39.0%	9	$182.25	$71.10
Teriyaki Chicken	$15.95	$3.19	20.0%	8	$127.60	$25.52
Shrimp and Scallop Pasta	$12.75	$3.87	30.4%	6	$76.50	$23.22
Barbecued Ribs	$14.50	$4.38	30.2%	14	$203.00	$61.32
Meatloaf	$9.25	$2.62	28.3%	11	$101.75	$28.82
Baked Pork Chop	$10.50	$3.22	30.7%	7	$73.50	$22.54
Fish and Chips	$8.95	$2.77	31.0%	10	$89.50	$27.70
Broiled Salmon Steak	$13.45	$4.07	30.3%	5	$67.20	$20.35
Totals				70	$921.30	$280.57
Total Menu Food Cost %						30.50%

Total costs divided by total income equals the ideal menu pre-cost percentage for the main menu items ($292.09 divided by $950.55 equals 30.7 percent ideal food cost). If you had projected that a 35 percent food cost would be profitable and if your predetermined mix of sales stays on this track, your business should be in good shape. However, if there is a preliminary indication that the projected mix will produce a food cost in excess of the budget, adjust the menu by including some lower cost items. If these are attractive enough to customers, you can divert sales to a more desirable mix. You need the difference between the 35 percent and the ideal menu pre-cost of 30.7 percent to compensate for those other hidden costs.

The projected unit sales are only an educated guess during the period before opening, but once you have some actual sales experience to use in this format, it will be evident how easy it is to calculate realistic data from the actual mix of sales. Most modern point-of-sale cash registers can be programmed to provide data for every meal service period. After opening your business, you can keep track of the menu mix from actual experience, so you can identify the impact of the sales mix on the overall food cost. At that point, you can benefit from some practical analysis. If these costs are out of line, adjust the menu, prices, or promotions accordingly to bring overall pre-costs more in line with the budget.

If it is determined that a projected cost percentage, including the added variables of major menu items, will exceed the required operational food cost, do not lose heart. There are still many opportunities to reach your objective. Absolutely do not try to cheapen the menu or reduce the quality of ingredients to reach the desired food cost. Always remember customers will be mainly attracted to your business because of excellent food at reasonable prices. Do not mess with that model. There are many other ways to reach your goal. Start making another list containing all the other potential items to include on the menu. These should have a positive effect on keeping overall food cost percentages down, since, compared to the entrees, most will be lower in cost relative to their selling prices. This is especially true for beverages of all kinds, with the exception of wines. Take the time to pre-cost every additional item so it can be priced properly, including appetizers, salads, sandwiches, and desserts.

Determine the total cost percentage of the projected sales of all the other menu items, and add that to the main menu item numbers. The impact from beverages in particular, which is a big number, will be significant, especially if alcoholic beverages are offered. In most cases, the revenue from other sales will give you the leeway needed to maintain main menu prices at competitive and customer-accepted levels. Take, for example, the following illustration, in which the main entree dinners are projected by preliminary calculations to exceed the food cost budget of 35 percent:

Projected Main Menu Sales Revenue	$10,000
Projected Main Menu Food Cost	$3,800
Food Cost %	38%
Projected Other Menu Sales Revenue	
Appetizers	$1,000
Desserts	$500
Beverages	$2,000
Total Other Revenue	$3,500
Projected Other Menu Food Cost	$875
Food Cost %	25%
Total Sales including other	$13,500
Total Food Cost including other	$4,675
Total Food Cost % ($4,675 / $13,500)	34.6%

Here is a projected overall 34.6 percent food cost, which is a hair under the necessary 35 percent the operation requires. It is always better to be a little under than over since some unexpected food cost crisis may be just around the corner. Add the variable costs of waste, spillage, and production errors into these calculations. In the above example, this factor was already determined and built into the pre-cost recipe calculations, but it can be done either way, before or after.

The entire process is a great deal of work but worth it, for this is a systematic calculation of the costs before opening a business. It may not be exact, but it is better than starting out blind. With advance calculations, there is a much higher probability of achieving targeted goals. Those who avoid the process of preplanning their menu price and cost projections and leave it to guesswork wind up disappointed when their profits fall short of expectations.

Completing a pre-cost analysis and establishing realistic menu prices is a good amount of work, but this is only the beginning of tracking the numbers and keeping on course. This is because nothing ever stays the same, especially the cost of food and the cost of all the other purchases necessary to keep an enterprise going. Make an inventory price list of all the necessary food and supply products to track changes in purchase costs. Get organized by creating a product category that relates to supplier invoices for easy data entry and tracking. Taking a market basket comparison of food purchasing costs from month to month is the best approach, which is the aggregate of all food needs for the period. There will be some increases and some decreases, but the most important factor is the net change to determine the total impact of combined purchasing.

For example, if purchasing costs for food have increased by 5 percent over the past three months, it is obvious that corrective action is needed. Something must be done, or the operation will have to absorb the cost increases, which will reduce profits an equal amount. Take heart, for you can investigate and apply any one or more of the following options:

1. One of the first places to look would be in every refrigerator in the food service operation. Piles of leftovers turning into waste due to over-production are the number one cause of runaway food costs. This is a common problem in poorly managed kitchens, where food production records are not kept up-to-date. A food production record is simply a system of forecasting food sales by menu item, based on sales history, to predict how much raw food you need to purchase and prepare.

2. Evaluate all menu prices and decide on a few selective price increases

that would be the least bothersome to customers. Rather than increasing any entrees, perhaps increasing some other category, such as beverage prices, would be in order.

3. Find ways to reduce costs by finding a less expensive source for the products you are currently using. Try not to lose quality with lower priced items.

4. Examine the operation for possible wasteful practices that are correctable:

   a. Inaccurate portion control.

   b. Not maintaining strict adherence to recipes.

   c. Overproduction or over-purchasing.

   d. Poor utilization of leftovers.

   e. Untrained employees.

   f. Lack of ample security.

5. Consider introducing and promoting a new menu item, which has a higher gross profit margin (same as lower food cost percentage). Train employees in suggestive selling and provide incentives and rewards for their efforts.

6. Eliminate an item that is too costly to produce but certainly not one that is quite popular with customers. It could cause disappointment among customers, which could induce a drop in sales.

7. Reduce costs in areas of your operation other than food. No one said holding to a food cost alone is the only key to making a profit. Examine labor productivity and direct expenses, which quite often slip away from daily scrutiny.

8. Add customer value to meal promotions by offering a combo deal. To the higher entree offer lower food cost additions, such as appetizers or desserts. Doing so will build up the check average.

9. Most customers are not too happy about adding costs to their high-priced entree by having to pay extra for a salad or a vegetable. By including a great salad bar and a variety of excellent fresh breads, customers get a sense they are receiving real value. Price the total package right and earn a fair profit.

10. Get excited and increase customer sales through promotions, advertising, catering, delivery, or whatever you believe will stimulate the top line. Creating higher sales is almost certainly the best long-term strategy of all.

I am stopping after 10, for it is time to start using your imagination and come up with your own original ideas for coping with rising costs. Success in this business depends largely on individual creativity.

Please note, it is not always a good thing to get overly excited about cost changes when they are a result of seasonal quirks and temporary shortages. Perhaps these variable cost blips should have been anticipated and taken into consideration when devising the overall financial plan. Also, there are sometimes windfalls of unexpected bargains and price dips, which in some ways will compensate for temporary cost increases. Stay on top of purchasing and take advantage of these opportunities when they come along to compensate for the negatives. If you can manage to take these fluctuations in stride without seriously affecting profits, it will serve you well to stay the course and not play with menu prices.

Nothing is more disturbing to customers than frequent price changes. There will also be the cost of re-writing the menu and retraining employees. The main things are to monitor the trends and to determine the permanent consequences of inflationary cost increases. When menu price changes must occur, do so as infrequently as possible and only after assessing the impact on customers' perceptions. However, after having done everything possible to avoid increasing prices, there comes a time to do it for the right reasons.

First, be certain that the items up for consideration reflect good value to the customer and that those items have not been increased for a reasonable length of time. Check out the competition for similar items within comparable service operations. Do not be so proud of the fact that your restaurant's prices are significantly lower and that is the reason customers return. Low menu pricing may be attracting some additional business, but you may be unwittingly giving up some potential profits because you are underpriced for the market. Know the competition well and compare not only their pricing, but their quality, portion sizes, and style of service. Quality comes first, especially when it comes to building and retaining repeat business. Premium menu pricing is a deterrent only if it does not reflect value.

When feeling reluctant to take the appropriate action, you should ask if you are willing to absorb cost increases and lower hard-earned profits for someone else's benefit. If cost increases cannot be compensated in any other way, that is exactly what will happen, and it will be due to the manager's indecision alone. Price increases are an economic fact of life, and if done intelligently, with good planning, and with the right timing, the risk of losing customer loyalty will be minimized — not eliminated entirely but certainly minimized to the extent that short-term losses of income will be more than compensated for by the long-term benefits. But do not wait too long; every day spent procrastinating costs money.

Recognize the fact that some customers are price conscious and may be vocal about even the slightest increase. This situation requires some backbone and confidence that you are following a well-thought-out business decision. You may be able to express some form of justification to placate the complainers, but if not, it is best to take it in stride and move on. Furthermore, it is a good bet that they will not complain to a successor who will undoubtedly follow with higher prices. Just stick with your plan.

The real value of pre-costing before rather than after opening your doors for business is the ability to price the menu with a high degree of accuracy. If the food cost percentage necessary to produce a profit was miscalculated and prices were set too low at the beginning, there will be a problem. Not only is the income lost from day one, but now you run the risk of losing customers by making substantial price increases. It may have made sense at the beginning that you could sustain low prices by attracting a high volume of customers, but if those sales do not materialize, you cannot afford to sustain those low prices and remain in business. This strategy seldom works. It is a wiser move to price the menu from the beginning according to basic customer value and realistic costs.

When no other choices are left and price changes must be made, be smart and do not try to do it all at once. It is best to be selective in raising only a limited number of prices to which customers are not super sensitive. Add some value specials to the menu that are less costly to produce. Try a theme promotion to tie in with seasonal holidays. Teach the staff to give a little more attention and service. Do some extra cleaning and replace or add some decorations. Above all, be insistent on great quality. This is the time to be at your best. If the job is done well, most customers will understand, and the fallout will be minimal.

Never leave the future of a business to chance. It is too much of a risk, and real money is at stake. The major food service concerns have developed built-in systems borne of many years of trial and experience. For the independent and new entrepreneurs, it is a tedious and difficult task but one that is essential if they want a good shot at predicting and controlling their future. Many years ago, my first supervisor, Mr. Ridley Smith, introduced me to one of his most successful managers, who made it his business to know his numbers. He knew the cost of all his purchased products, knew the cost of every item on his menu, became involved in the process, kept track of it, and therefore was able to adjust his operation accordingly. It required work and planning, but the effort paid off. It was a good lesson to learn early in my career, and I believe it served me well in my progress up the line. The emphasis bears repeating today: If you are going to be successful in this business, you must know your numbers.

Chapter 4

Labor Cost Control

(Taking the mystery out of managing your most vital asset.)

The first and most emphatic directive that I received from my superiors concerning making a profit in the food management business was to above all control my labor costs. The meaning of that is open to interpretation and means different things to different people. It all depends on your point of view and how you choose to address the problem. To the accountants and absentee owners of the world, it means keeping those labor cost percentages within budget, and they do not care how it gets done. The other related problems of productivity and good customer service are not their concern, at least for the moment.

To a new manager on the job, it might mean not hiring anyone over the minimum wage, providing few benefits, and freezing all raises. To a more experienced manager, it could mean hiring the best people possible, paying them well, and letting productivity and good service take care of itself. Someone else might take the view of hiring all new people at low rates, providing an intensive training program, and developing them the company's way. All these approaches have good and bad points. There is no single concept that will work at all times, and it may take a variety of approaches, depending heavily on the judgment of the operating managers.

Before setting a policy for employment and controlling labor costs, you must first take into consideration the kind of business you will be operating. Table service, cafeteria, fast food, diners, and catering all require different talents and levels of experience. Depending on the type of business, first know what the market is doing and what competitors are paying their employees. If involved in any kind of interviewing, you should be able to get a feel for competitive pay scales, since most applicants, if prompted, will reveal their hourly earnings on previous jobs. However, be sure to do some cross-checking to confirm what is said, because some applicants are inclined to exaggerate to establish a higher starting pay. When in doubt, it is always a good idea to do some investigating. Most competitors are not willing to share information and if contacted will certainly be on their guard. At least try to ascertain the availability and the pay scales of various levels of food service jobs by getting involved with the local restaurant association. Often, labor costs will turn out to be everyone's number one problem.

If managers can remember the one thing that is most critical to keeping labor costs under control, it is to understand that it all starts at the point of hire. It may sound simplistic and easier said than done, but the hiring process is where most fail to put forth the necessary effort. Some are either too busy to take the time or impatiently hiring the first one or two applicants who show up at the door. If it is a large enough business to afford a human resources department, use it fully, for those personnel can render the operating managers a valuable, timesaving service. It should be a cooperative process, where human resources assumes the time-consuming task for seeking the employee candidates needed. However, it should be the responsibility of the frontline manager to conduct the final interview and make the final hiring decision.

The human resources people are good at taking on the work load of recruiting, screening, taking care of the paperwork, and making sure the process complies with all the employment laws. They should be good at attracting and screening the employees that you clearly specify in writing. If a cook is needed, the manager needs to describe the level of experience required and the specific skills necessary for that particular job. If the job specifications are clearly outlined, it will save management from wasting its time interviewing candidates who do not meet the minimum qualifications. However, when time runs short and hiring needs become critical, management by expediency occurs too often. It is a trap formed by not being prepared ahead of time. If unprepared, you have little choice but to take whomever shows up. Of course, when the new hire cannot perform, there is the problem of either retraining, which requires more management time, or possibly termination, at which point the process starts all over again.

This cycle of turnover is a direct road to business failure and even more so in a service business that depends so highly on customer satisfaction. Perhaps, even with the best recruiting programs, not every new employee works out, but by making it a priority, chances for success are improved. Putting management time and effort into the hiring process produces one of the best returns on investment that can be made in almost any industry.

The competence of employees is the most critical factor that determines the ultimate success of a business. It should be apparent that this is where the most effort should be concentrated. It requires a constant investment in time, patience, and energy. However, due to the transient nature of food service, it is easy to become discouraged and somewhat cynical about spending effort on people who may not be around too long. Beware of this defeatist attitude, and do not give in to it. Accepting high turnover rates and the resulting poor productivity is a recipe for failure. Successful businesses have learned the importance of investing in their personnel practices, and studies have proven that low employee turnover equates to long-term profitability in an industry known for its high failure rate.

Therefore, enlightened managers make the recruiting and development of their employees a priority. They understand how winning sports teams achieve what they do and why they invest their time and money into recruiting the best talent possible. Such a good idea deserves to be copied.

The universal concern for most food service operators is where good employees can be found. One of the best potential resources for career food service personnel that is often overlooked is the vocational school system. Here are young people in training who have dreams of becoming successfully employed but who have difficulties making the right connections. There are two major problems. The industry is not always aware of this resource to take advantage of it, and most are not prepared with a development plan for new recruits at this entry level.

Youngsters at this point in their lives need more attention than seasoned workers do, and more important, they need a future to believe in. Young people tend to be idealistic, and to some extent, may have unrealistic views of the real world. At some time, most of us have been there and should understand when aspiring recruits are placed in tough situations for the first time. It can be too rough an adjustment for some to handle. This is the point where attitudes can quickly go sour, and what could have been a promising future for someone is lost forever. Young people on their first job are at a delicate stage, but if approached and led in the right manner, they can pay back their new employers with superb effort and loyalty. However, it is up to the employer to put forth some effort to earn it. A sincere mentoring process needs to be effectively in place, where personal attention and support is a real commitment. Bringing a young person along takes more time and faith in his or her potential, but the effort and the results can be rewarding.

It does not always work out the way you expect, and the young person sometimes goes elsewhere for work. No one bats a thousand, but in terms of percentage, you will be well ahead of the game and the competition.

Even if a few leave, you may still be a recipient of some residual rewards. People who are treated well have good memories. Some may return with even greater skills, for they recall the optimism and your belief in their futures. Others may send fresh candidates, for they know that people are treated right. If nothing else, you have earned a reputation for developing young people for careers in this industry, and that is deserving of high praise. It is a mind-set worthy of good leadership.

It would be naive to believe that it is possible to hire perfectly qualified personnel for all positions that need filling. Since few new hires are not 100 percent effective at the start, it will always be necessary to have ample orientation and training programs in place. The emphasis needs to be just as much on the thorough orientation of a new employee as the training itself. Training addresses the skill aspect, but orientation addresses the development of attitude. Here again is where management needs to invest an adequate amount of time.

The immediate needs for any new employee are acceptance and a clear understanding of what is expected. There is a window of opportunity to set new employees on the right track, and management needs to be aware that this window quickly closes. During the first few days on the job, new employees are most likely to accept direction and are more willing to pay close attention to company policies than at any other time. They will also feel welcome and more accepted if someone in command takes the time to show them the ropes. It is the opportune time when the seeds of a good service attitude can be planted, and then with continued good care, successfully grown and flourished. If you fail to pay close attention to new employees because you are too busy, they can easily become discouraged and frustrated with their new job if it is not clear what is expected. Certainly you do not want them to fall prey to those chronic complainers who may be lurking somewhere in the operation. These malcontents are more than willing to indoctrinate the new kids on the block in their ways, which can easily lead to the development of bad habits, or worse, a bad attitude.

Good managers know that orientation and new employee training is the right thing to do, but in practice, most food service operators will have difficulty finding the time to do it well. There is, however, a clever strategy. Many sharp operators have thought this through, and as a matter of policy, designate a few select employees, depending on the size of the business, who can act as a big brother or big sister to new employees. Those chosen are capable and are endowed with enthusiastic dispositions and a generous amount of patience. These are star performers who contribute immensely to the success of the business, the kind of people you want all employees to emulate.

The duration of the orientation and training process needs to be tailored to the individual and the level of skill involved. This is best accomplished by having direct, one-on-one sessions with the new employee to determine the level of progress that is desired and to review what exactly constitutes satisfactory performance. Sometimes it may lead to a decision that another assignment would be more appropriate, or it may reveal that the new person does not seem to fit anywhere. If the latter be the case, it is better the separation come early and save all those concerned some time and grief.

Having been given the designation as "trainer" is always a boost to an employee's morale and self-esteem, but of course, some additional material reward for the extra effort is also appreciated. Giving this responsibility to one of the best employees does not get the manager off the hook entirely, but it does give him or her the time to tend to other duties. The important thing is to be sure to follow up and monitor the progress of the new recruit. Every employee appreciates some personal interest from the boss, and the positive payback to the business is immeasurable.

Scores of articles have been written concerning the productivity of labor, and it seems to be the crying call of the past decade. World competition, downsizing, and the displacement of workers have devastated the American workplace and have made employees less loyal to their employers. Many simply fear for the security of their jobs, and this atmosphere literally forces people to look out for themselves first. This conflict certainly does not contribute to a productive employment atmosphere. Management can help to overcome some of these concerns by building more job security for their employees through better personnel practices. By hiring the right people for the job and by providing good training and opportunities for growth, job security can be made more attainable. To avoid the constant turmoil of employment turnover and personnel displacement, there must be responsibility for better planning, and that lies with management. There certainly are plenty of good reasons for employment terminations if a business is going to outlast the competition. What is uncalled for, however, is the reckless hiring of excessive personnel when it is unnecessary and then having to cull them when it is finally determined the business is overstaffed. The key is to determine labor requirements more accurately by pre-planning work schedules that closely meet the demands of production and service. The formula that reflects productivity best in food service are the sales in dollars divided by hours worked that tells how many sales are produced for every hour worked.

Each style of service requires a different level of productivity, mainly relating to the complexity of the meals being produced and the level of service expected by the customer. For example, a table-service dinner restaurant can expect more customers on Friday and Saturday evenings; therefore, more employee work hours need to be scheduled. This sounds simple, but the question is how many and what level of productivity is needed. Most managers do it by sight and feel, and often can do it well because of their experience. That is fine when all employees are working at their peak, but the "management by feel" method does not control costs consistently over a long time.

Since every operation is unique, there are few universal rules to follow. Before determining what high productivity for any operation is, first develop statistics through some old-fashioned trial-and-error techniques.

This may sound blasphemous, but in reality, it is a scientific approach based on experience factors for a specific situation.

The first trial is to apply judgment and schedule personnel so that the quality of service best meets the demands of customers for each day the business is open. Attempt to schedule for maximum efficiency, with a reserve or two for emergencies. You do not want customer service to suffer during this fact-finding procedure. Observe what is happening during, before, and after these service hours. Ask questions and keep notes on what is happening. The kitchen crew should be on the hustle but not overtaxed to the point of making errors or not getting the food out in time. Employees should be proficient in their duties. Make assignment changes or provide some additional training to take care of any problems. Servers must be taking good care of the customers, moving quickly throughout the serving period, without definite gaps caused by employees wasting time. Try to make sure there is just enough pressure to create an energetic atmosphere without sacrificing a quality experience for the customers. This is the time to record the facts and to fine-tune the scheduling. Some modification of employee assignments and additional training will be required.

Daily cram sessions during this trial period with employees in production and service areas will help sharpen the team and encourage cooperation. Share plans about analyzing productivity with employees. They are often closer to the work details than management and can be resourceful about solving problems and finding ways to do things better. Sometimes it is a simple matter of communication and eliminating roadblocks. They want to be successful just as much as management, because a successful operation means chances for better pay and the opportunity for advancement. Most of all, give them a feeling of respect, for that turns into self-motivation and a positive work environment. This entire process of research and analysis may take two to three weeks, depending on the complexity of the operation and how quickly decent refinements can be made. When the level of productivity appears to be at its peak, it is time to record exactly the hours of work that are required by the hour and day of the week. Take those hours and divide them into the sales that were recorded by the hour and day of the week as well. This will indicate the sales dollars that are generated by every hour and every day of input.

For example:

(Business open 5 p.m. to 10 p.m.) Friday Night Sales	$3,600
(Not including management) Total hours worked	125
Sales divided by hours worked equals Sales per Hour Worked	$ 28.80

Therefore, from an extensive analysis of Friday night's business, the indication is that $28.80 of sales produced for each hour worked is the target for peak productivity. Other days and other meal periods will reflect different amounts. This is a reflection of operating efficiency, which is the sales produced for each hour worked. This should be the standard target and be of assistance in preparing staffing schedules. By keeping daily records, productivity can be tracked on a daily basis. This is important when sales decline due to seasonal fluctuations or other factors, and adjustments, if not made, will result in lower sales per hour worked. A serious decline in sales per hour worked is a warning signal that management needs to be aware of, and prompt action must be taken if profit goals are to be met.

When sales are rising, productivity also rises, and that makes everyone look good. Do not be so concerned with tight staffing when higher sales cover up a multitude of sins. It is the decline in sales that calls for tough-minded management to take the appropriate action and to take it quickly. An operation might look good, even exceeding expectations, when several great dinner nights bring in additional revenue and higher profits. However, there may be one or more dinner periods when productivity is not being closely controlled, because the big nights are more than compensating for the slow ones. The week may look good, but it would be better if the slow nights were kept on track as well with proper scheduling according to service requirements. Even when times are good and profits are flush, if an opportunity to make profits is lost due to overstaffing, those profits are lost forever.

The productivity principal of sales per hour worked can be applied to almost all types of food service operations. For some institutional markets, using the number of meals served in place of sales is just as good a reference point. In all instances, the measurement reflects what is produced for every hour worked. Seasonal factors will greatly affect how efficient any food service operation can be managed. When circumstances are such that service must be provided even during slow periods or when patron population is low, there is still a productivity standard that can apply. It is during these situations that management can be creative by adjusting the style or manner of service to minimize the cost of labor. Some of these can be fun to do, like when one innovative manager had customers participate in preparing and serving their own meals. Some of these ideas have been well received in the institutional market, such as self-service buffets, grilling your own burgers to preference, frying one's own eggs, making your own waffles, self-service soup and salad bars, and build-your-own sundaes. The opportunities are limited only by the operator's imagination.

Wages and salaries are only part of the total labor cost picture. Taxes and other ancillary costs can be of major significance as well and need to be part of the labor cost budget plan. Be sure to keep up to date on the latest Social Security and Medicare taxes, which often change each year. You may not have much control over these, but you do have some control over the rates you are charged for unemployment and worker's compensation taxes. These are not insignificant, and they can have a dramatic bearing on the outcome of profit results. Unemployment taxes are regulated by the number of employees each business terminates for one reason or another. Here again, management that does a good job in hiring and retaining the right kind of employees will enjoy the least amount of government-assigned costs for unemployment taxes. Worker's compensation relates directly to the number of accidents that lead to employee injuries occurring at each business location. When management takes its responsibilities seriously to provide good training and a safe environment in which to work, these charges can also be kept to a minimum.

One of my first encounters with a new assignment was listening to my manager conduct an employee meeting where the key subject was safety in the kitchen. He did not talk as much about lost time and the expense as he did about the pain and suffering caused by an injury and that it can sometimes lead to a long-term disability. From my observation, it seemed to hit home with the employees. For some time afterward it was a rare occurrence for an accident or injury to occur. This experience taught me a valuable lesson on how to communicate and to tell people what matters by making it personal.

Here is a final note about pay scales in the food service industry. It is mainly a self-imposed and disgraceful situation that has penalized this field of business with a poor image, and it has severely influenced its ability to attract bright and ambitious people. I refer not to the entry-level hourly rates, which are appropriate, but to the false ceiling of material opportunities for the highly skilled and experienced workers. There are a few exceptions for the great chefs who can command high salaries, but for the majority of cooks, bakers, and salad makers, the opportunity to earn a decent living is limited. It is no small wonder the shortage of real talent is so prevalent. Not many are eager to pursue an occupation with such a negative reputation for low pay, as nobody wants to work hard when there are income limits. Some will advance further up the line into management positions, but the servers and the kitchen crews are the ones this business most heavily relies on.

Many say they cannot afford better pay and benefits for skilled food service workers, but perhaps that is the crux of the problem. By not having highly productive personnel in the kitchens, managers are inviting inconsistent performance, wasted steps, substandard quality, and the need for more expensive supervisory management. Those who have worked in a high-pressure kitchen environment can attest to the fact that two highly skilled and efficient food preparation employees can work circles around three mediocre ones.

Successful business leaders make their money by attracting customers, providing consistent quality, and by giving great service, not by paying cheap wages. You should not limit yourself based on an arbitrary idea about pay scales because that is what everybody else is doing. Perhaps when the industry matures further, it will come to recognize that, if food service operations are to be long-term successes, they will also have to provide better compensation and growth opportunities for their best employees by making it possible for them to succeed long-term as well.

Chapter 5

The Other Costs

(It is a long list you cannot afford to overlook.)

After all the time and attention given to controlling the two major categories of food and labor costs, it would be foolhardy to overlook the "other costs" that can have a strong effect on profitability. There are more than you might think, and individually they need to be scrutinized on a regular basis if they are to be kept under control. Some are not considered that important by management, but some can make a lasting impression on customers. A lack of investment or focus in certain areas can unwittingly inhibit sales growth and discourage repeat business. The following are some of the other costs that we need to pay close attention to.

Paper and Plastic Supplies

Depending on the type of operation, particularly for fast food and food services that provide carryout, these items can amount to major costs. Regular inventories should be made to determine an exact cost of usage for each period — at a minimum monthly. Take a good look at some storage rooms; they can be disaster areas, overloaded with a variety of out-of-date products because management could not make up its mind as to what to use. Since it is necessary to purchase these products in large quantities, it is important that well-thought-out decisions are made before large orders are placed. If you are unsure whether a new disposable product is going to work, it would be wise to experiment with some samples before committing to a new program. Most suppliers are willing to be of assistance, and if you attend trade shows to see what is new on the market, purveyors will often work with you in anticipation of a future sale. The key is not to make any quick decisions until a plan is thought through; otherwise, the storage room will turn into an overstuffed junk room.

Monogramming napkins or cups with the business name or to promote a mascot can easily be done with some moderate initial up-front costs, and over time, the markup cost on purchases is minimal. Many managers feel this adds a little class to their operation and helps to increase name recognition.

Signs

The big difference between the chains and the independents is the ability of the chains to spend the big bucks on signs, external and internal. Of course they can afford to make the investment, and they also know from practical experience that customers are attracted to good signs. Professionally done signs present an image that communicates pride in the name and implies a sense of permanence. It says, "We're proud of who we are, and we're here to stay." The independents, especially the smaller ones, are short of cash and often settle for something far less extravagant. Perhaps they have no other choice, but if they consider the big picture, a good investment in the beginning will more than pay for itself in the long run. In the real world of competition today, strong name recognition and signs in good taste will help get attention.

Restrooms

Restrooms can provide one of the best returns on money. However, when it comes to installing a first-class restroom, some operators seem to give it a low priority. Many customers measure the status of an establishment based on the quality of its restrooms. Customers are turned off by meagerly appointed restrooms and poorly maintained facilities. Installing an outstanding restroom facility can justify adding 2 percent to menu prices without customers even noticing. It is warranted because people appreciate an exceptional facility and absolutely want one that is kept immaculately clean. What is good for customers is equally good for employees. Doing the right thing in this area shows respect for employees and offers a better chance that the area will be properly maintained. Neglecting your responsibility to provide a well equipped and supplied facility is an invitation to abuse and places good health practices and sanitation in jeopardy.

Cleaning Supplies

Like paper and plastic supplies, the category of cleaning supplies can become costly if not controlled. It is important to take a regular inventory of all cleaning products to ascertain correct usage and determine total costs. A way to portion out these items needs to be implemented, because most employees, left uninstructed, give little thought to how much they should use of each cleaning chemical. They think that if a little does a good job, twice as much will do even better. Unfortunately, when people erroneously think that way, it ends up costing money. A pot washer in my employ at one time, thinking more was better, used four times as much cleaning powder as was necessary. The pot washer conveniently kept a 60-pound storage barrel of detergent next to the sink and was using a two-quart pot to scoop the product into the wash compartment. Our first step was to move the storage barrel back to the store room and then give the pot washer an adequate quantity each day, along with a properly sized measuring scoop. We even explained the reason for doing it correctly and gave him a good measure of encouragement. It was amazing how quickly things got better, and our cost of detergent was dramatically reduced.

In recent years, the better distributors of cleaning supplies are willing to install, at no additional charge, devices that will dispense the correct amount of the cleaning chemical needed for the specific job at hand. By all means, take advantage of these services. If dishes are cleaned using an automatic dishwasher, this becomes even more critical. Be sure that the supplier, whether the machine is owned or leased, maintains the equipment so that only the exact amount of detergent necessary is used to clean and sanitize wares. To neglect this area can result in some significant costs that are not always apparent, and your hard-earned profits will be literally going down the drain.

Utilities

Save some money and do not turn on all the lights, stoves, ovens, and fryers when starting the day. Unnecessary energy is wasted when this occurs. Granted, there are some things that should be on, but if you give it some practical thought and set up a reasonable system, it is a good bet you could save at least 10 percent annually on utility bills. Get in touch with the utility company, as it will be happy to offer some free advice on utility savings. Also, there are companies who, for a modest charge, will make an energy efficiency study of the operation and provide a comprehensive plan to help minimize costs. Some physical changes may be called for, but before taking a big risk, first evaluate cost savings versus investment. The same goes for purchasing or replacing equipment in the facility. Review the power usage and efficiency ratings that can have a considerable effect on utility expenditures over time. Some of these things may seem trivial compared to all the other factors of operating a business, but for the professional manager who is always looking to improve profitability, there are some worthwhile savings to uncover in this area.

Repairs and Maintenance

Nothing hurts more than an unexpected repair expenditure. For those who do not want to bother with preventative maintenance, it is a question of whether you want to pay now or later, and paying later will hurt a lot more. If you do not have the resources or the personnel to make repairs yourself, it makes sense to consider a maintenance contract. It does cost money, but the assurance of keeping an operation running every day with a degree of reliability can do wonders for peace of mind. In the end, it will save money. Some operators would rather save the expense and do it themselves, which is fine as long as you have the time to read and understand the manuals and have all the proper tools. At a minimum, though, any number of routine preventative maintenance tasks should be do-able. When purchasing new equipment, be sure to carefully review and understand the warranties. Take advantage of suppliers, who can provide training for employees when purchasing new equipment. Also, most manufacturers will provide training videos that demonstrate the correct usage and cleaning of their products, which is imperative for keeping the costly investment as maintenance-free as possible. A valuable side benefit is that when employees know how to use and clean equipment properly, they are more inclined to take care of it with a sense of pride and safety.

Office Equipment

Every business that intends to succeed should have an up-to-date, computerized office setup. Having a hodgepodge collection of dated equipment will not only be unserviceable, but also will reflect poorly on the image of the business. Granted, a startup business cannot afford top of the line, but you must have at minimum a basic system. When investment finances are slim, there are leasing options, and most come with complete service arrangements. Leasing copying machines is a good example. Pens, pencils, pads, marking pens, tape dispensers, staplers, and numerous other office expendables can disappear quite easily. No one takes anything intentionally, but without some semblance of control, the expenditures for these items can become remarkably high. Start out by setting up an adequate supply, but be sure to keep replacements securely locked away. Avoid the invitation for these items to start traveling, and assign someone the responsibility for issuing and control. Give them some power, back them up, and they will love it. Never give this assignment to a management person who should have other important things to do.

Service Ware

Dishware, glasses, eating utensils, and all the miscellaneous items necessary to provide customers with the best is a big investment. How well these assets are maintained will determine how much it will cost for replacements over time. Many who start out with some fine service ware find that their replacement costs become prohibitive, and they are forced to downgrade the quality of their service ware before reordering. Because replacement costs can easily mount from 1 to 2 percent of total annual sales, which significantly affects the bottom line, the challenge for management is how breakage and losses can be reduced to a minimum. Educating and training the workforce seems to be an effective solution and is certainly worth the effort. One manager who experienced a lot of breakage and loss cleverly assembled a four-by-eight ply poster board and attached one of each service ware item used in the operation with the cost visibly printed beside each one. This poster was prominently displayed in a high-traffic area for all employees to observe. Written below the poster was an appeal to be careful and a note about how excessive costs to replace these service ware items had a direct impact on the ability of the business to pay the employees. The manager reported that, within a short amount of time, the losses declined by more than 50 percent. As promised, the employees were rewarded appropriately when the time came for their annual wage review. The episode was a good example of how employees, when informed about what constitutes cost and how their behavior can affect it, will cooperate when it serves their best interests.

The Trash

The trash may be an afterthought, but herein lies what can be a serious leakage problem. When individuals are careless and want to avoid embarrassment, they sometimes try to hide their mistakes. For this reason some food service operators do not even allow automatic garbage disposals in their kitchens because it is too easy for kitchen personnel to dispose of usable products as well as botched items. Keeping a eye open as to what goes on in every section of the kitchen operation is the first line of defense. Periodically inspecting trash stations in the kitchen areas will indicate if food production personnel are excessively trimming raw products, throwing away overproduction, or not completely emptying food containers. When the trash leaves the building it would be wise for someone in management to know what is being discarded. Every day you may find a fork, a spoon, or a small serving dish that has accidentally fallen into the trash can from the soiled dish scrapping area. It does not sound like much, but it can add up to big money if it occurs on a daily basis. This is especially true in large institutional kitchens where there is a considerable volume of service ware processed three times a day. Since the items are often low cost, no one seems to think it matters much. But some steps should be taken to minimize these preventable losses.

Bug Control

The evidence of roaches and other vermin in a food service operation is enough to make you ill. New and old facilities are equally vulnerable to these pests, and what is most frustrating is they can be just as evident in operations that practice the highest standards of sanitation. In most instances, they thrive in a dark environment where water does not drain away completely, a problem for many kitchens with crowded equipment and constant dampness. If these pests are not brought under control, they multiply and keep moving around to various hiding places. If you encounter a problem of this nature, now is not a time to seek out the exterminator with the lowest bid. Many small exterminating businesses have popped up claiming to be knowledgeable but are rather slow on producing results. Their normal service schedule is monthly, where some poison — that usually stinks up the place while killing off only a few of the critters on the surface — is spread around. One or two dead ones does not guarantee the exterminating process has reached the source of their breeding. It can be a long, drawn-out procedure that never improves, and your local bug man will be quick to provide numerous excuses, from blaming the local climate to the bug's ability to build up a resistance to the latest chemicals. Do not buy into this nonsense. The job can be done completely if you are willing to deal with a reputable firm that will do the job right and provide written guarantees. It is not cheap but worthwhile when measured against a bad health inspection report or a customer who finds a bug in his or her salad. Be prepared to do it right, and you will not regret it.

Advertising

No matter how confident you are about the appeal of your dining services and your ability to draw patron sales through word of mouth, never underestimate the power of advertising. Freedom of choice and a plethora of new and attractive food choices is the reality in today's marketplace. Competition is increasing, which ultimately means someone is always trying to steal your business. To be the leader of the pack, do everything possible to get your good name spread around. It does not mean you have to break the bank, but be realistic and budget a reasonable percentage of sales income to some form of advertising; some advise between 1 and 2 percent. How extensive it is depends on your ideas and creativity. It can range anywhere from a simple ad in the local newspaper or magazine to a personal interview on television touting the magnificence of the menu. Sponsoring community events and participating in food shows and culinary events can get you some excellent name recognition and a reputation for being civic-minded. Anything to attract positive attention to a business and its employees is a form of advertising. The smart businessperson does not take tomorrow's sales for granted. Yesterday's sales are already in the bank, but tomorrow's are going to the promoters who are constantly seeking out those new customers.

The above list should cover most of the major, direct expenses in running a food service operation, but there are a few other cost items that should be mentioned. They include the telephone, licenses, insurance, and taxes other than sales taxes. Though these items may seem minor, do not let them get out of control. They must be accounted for and included in the budget. Beyond the direct operating expenses for conducting business, and depending on what aspect of commerce you are operating in, there still may be more to consider.

One rather large item is the rent for the operating space. If this expense exceeds 10 percent of the sales income, there may be trouble. To warrant a rental cost beyond this limit, you would have to make an extremely low food cost relative to sale prices. One example would be concession sales at sporting events and recreational parks where the consumer expects to pay extraordinary prices for refreshments because it is traditionally part of the overall deal. For the entertainment complex, concessionaire rents are an important part of its overall income. Having a business in a mall is another example where high rents are readily justified by the mall owners who claim the mall attracts many additional customers, including the advantages of parking, lighting, and signs. This is true to a point, but still the burden lies heavily on the independent business owner to attract and keep those customers. When some malls begin to lose their market appeal, a leased business might have to disband or move elsewhere if it cannot sustain the cost of the lease and still make ends meet. Other than these exceptions, high rent can be the singular downfall for many businesses that otherwise would be successful. Negotiating the appropriate lease at the right price for a business can be the chief factor in whether the business will survive or not.

Institutional and industrial enterprises should also appropriate a certain amount of space and invest in facilities that provide the necessary service required by their constituents. Therefore, it warrants including this as a line item expense; otherwise it becomes buried in the category labeled "overhead." The fewer overhead expenses needing justification, the better. It is more realistic to assign all expenditures where they ultimately belong, so everyone sees the true picture of what auxiliary services cost.

Finally, the crux of any venture lies in the financial investment and the level of debt that must be assumed to maintain a business venture. Every business must have a plan and anticipate how much debt is affordable based on projected sales, while still providing an adequate income for the owner. All loaning institutions will require a realistic business plan with substantial evidence that repayment is guaranteed before ever approving a loan. New ventures may attract private investors who are willing to take more risks, but they also want a bigger piece of the pie when profits are eventually divided. Being realistic beforehand and being prepared for the rigors of acquiring adequate financing is the mark of an astute businessperson. Those who are not experts in this area should hire professional counsel.

Identifying and accounting for all "other costs" will require digging deep, but they are better addressed beforehand than unpleasantly discovered later on. Be a planner, be competent, and be well armed up front with the full knowledge of what comprises all the detailed expenditures involved in operating a business. Be mindful that there is forever something or someone around the corner ready to increase your costs or steal away your profits, so be prepared for those inevitable circumstances.

Chapter 6

The Profit & Loss Statement

(Staying on track with a monthly statement.)

If you are unsure where you are going on a monthly basis, chances are you are going in the wrong direction. Ignorance is not bliss when it comes to running a business, and it is amazing how many managers and business owners today do not have a clue what profit and loss track they are on. Perhaps they gauge their profit or loss for the month by the balance in their checking account. If sales are good and the money is coming in, why worry?

Anticipating and planning a course of action to deal with the changing course of events is the mark of a manager on top of his or her game. You have to keep asking the right questions about the future. Figure out how to deal with a downturn of events. If you know from experience that sales decline during certain seasons of the year, plan how to react, or better yet, plan ahead. Observe trends and evaluate ways to circumvent the inevitable problems of cost increases and competition. This information is critical to keeping a business on the right track. Finding out about problems and taking action too late often leads to disaster.

Most major chains have accountability systems in place that report detailed monthly and even weekly costs up the chain of command. It is a must. Higher management is measured by results, and that means profit and loss tracking systems need to work sooner, not later. The system has, in a sense, its own built-in worry machine. When numbers begin to go astray, managers in the field are put on alert. Corrective action plans that have been thought out in advance are promptly put into effect. It is one of the better attributes of a large, well-managed organization. Individual operators often do not have the benefit of such built-in profit control systems. Many feel that because they are so close to their business on a daily basis, they are in a secure position to keep an "eye on things." However, sometimes the underlying problems may not be so evident. Lurking under the surface lie the facts and the real numbers.

Depending on an accountant can be fine, but an accountant can give back an operational report based only on the information you provided in the first place. Feedback may be based on operational data two or three months old. That is way too late to keep on top of things and effectively correct problems. Even the smallest of operators must have more timely information. Keeping track of your own numbers is not that difficult, but it takes a little time and effort — that is, if you are not too tired from the daily tasks of food prep, serving customers, and taking out the trash. If time is consumed with tasks that would be better assigned to an hourly employee, a manager has abdicated his or her duty. Do not slip into unproductive situations that will severely drain time and energy. Step back occasionally and realize what is going on and why the business exists in the first place. It is about making money, and it helps to know what the numbers mean.

There was a time during my checkered career when I was in the commercial real estate business brokering the buying and selling of small to medium restaurants. The turnover was simply amazing and even more so the number of people who get into this business with no idea what they are doing. For whatever reason — and mostly the wrong ones — countless inexperienced and ill-prepared people venture forth into business. I admire their courage, but it is sad and unfortunate not only for the failed owners but for the public who have had to suffer through some awful experiences of poor quality and service. The public eventually responds by serving due justice. They stop going, and the business ultimately fails.

In almost every instance in which a restaurant was up for sale, the reason was primarily too much work and too little money. The financial rewards for all the hard work and long hours were not there, which eventually forced the owner to sell. Trying to extract financial information from sellers was difficult, since most of the owners kept few records with any semblance of order. Food cost data was a mystery. Asking about pertinent statistical data was like inquiring about something in a foreign language. Basic operating numbers are needed in order to establish the value of the business. When a business is up for sale, certain financial documents are necessary to confirm to potential buyers actual profit performance to justify the asking price. This is called due diligence.

After some friendly arm-twisting a seller's accountant eventually was able to assemble and submit a basic history of sales and cost information. While reviewing these financial records it was routinely observed that the cost of goods sold, or "food cost," widely varied from month to month. It was obvious that inventories were never taken, so it was impossible to track an accurate food cost except as an average over a long time. Without this essential information, the owners did not have a clue if they were on or off budget. Therefore, they had no control or ability to take corrective measures on a timely basis to avoid profit losses. These owners were relying solely on the cash accounting system, which does not offer any more information than how much is left over in their bank account at the end of the month. For some, this system is sufficient as long as the business is going well and total sales continue to exceed total costs. However, the marketplace does not usually work that way, and when the money runs out, it is too late to react and make the necessary corrections. What is hard for many restaurant owners to admit is that they never had any control over their product cost in the first place because they never knew what their numbers were at any specific point in time. The only way they could have calculated their actual food cost was to have taken a systematic and consistent monthly inventory of food and supplies. The formula is simple:

Beginning Inventory plus Purchases minus Ending Inventory equals Cost of Goods Sold.

$$\text{Or } (Inv.1 + P - Inv. 2 = Cost)$$

For example:

Beginning Inventory	$3,000
Plus Purchases +	$7,000
Total	$10,000
Minus Ending Inventory -	$2,500
Equals Costs of Goods Sold	$7,500

An accurate cost of goods sold is an exact accounting of what raw materials were consumed for the period. It is the cost of food, beverages, or whatever was required to generate sales for a specific time, whether it is weekly or monthly. It is important to accurately calculate this cost on a regular basis for the following reasons:

1. Food is the major cost category for a restaurant operation, and it is the primary basis for the profitability of a business.

2. Even minor cost changes will dramatically affect profitability (If the business earns 5 percent profit a year after all costs and expenses, a 1 percent deviation in food cost will raise or lower profit by 20 percent (one-fifth).

3. Higher cost over budget may indicate purchase price increases, overproduction, waste, inaccurate portion control, theft, or other leaks that should require prompt investigation and correction.

4. Lower cost under budget may indicate the customer is being shortchanged, inferior products being used, or an inaccurate inventory count.

5. It provides an accurate basis for comparison with other similar businesses, industry norms, and overall changes that may need to occur as other cost categories of a business change, such as payroll costs and rent.

Taking inventory at least once per month to calculate food cost does not necessarily need to be a time-consuming chore. The important thing is to be organized and consistent. First, establish what to count and at what units of measure: pounds, boxes, or each. Do not count every last bean. Count the major cost ingredients such as meats, poultry, fish, canned, frozen, and fresh. Separate them in such a manner so that they coincide with their location in the kitchen, and inventory can proceed systematically. You may count the same item stored in separate locations, so leave room in the column to make more than one pencil notation. It is not necessary to count miscellaneous condiments, bread, spices, and partially opened boxes and cans unless they amount to a significant value. Count the same things in the same way every time.

The following illustration contains a limited number of items in a sample inventory format:

Item	Unit	Cost	Count	Total Cost
Top Round of Beef	Lb.	$2.45	40	$98
Whole Pork Loin	Lb.	$2.15	65	$139.75
Chicken Breast	Lb.	$2.12	30	$63.60
Frozen Halibut Steaks	Lb.	$6.65	20	$133
6 oz. Hamburger Patties	Lb.	$1.91	52	$99.32
Swiss Cheese	Lb.	$1.88	15	$28.20
Gargonzola	Lb.	$2.71	8	$21.68
Cheddar Cheese	Lb.	$2.62	21	$55.02
Iceberg Lettuce	Case	$18.55	1.5	$27.83
Romaine	Bunch	$0.95	6	$5.70
Tomatoes	Flat	$14.25	1.3	$18.53
Russet Potatoes	50 Lb. Sack	$22.45	0.5	$11.23
Fresh Green Beans	Bushel	$14.45	0.5	$7.23
Mayonnaise	Gal.	$2.88	6	$17.28
Catsup	#10 Can	$3.45	7	$24.15
Diced Tomatoes	#10 Can	$3.34	14	$46.76
Peach Halves	#10 Can	$3.92	3	$11.76
Total Cost of Inventory				$809.04

This basic form can be developed on a spreadsheet program, such as Excel. It can be tailored to fit your specific needs and for any type of operation. The beauty of the computer spreadsheet is that it will calculate all the extensions and totals quickly and accurately. When purchase prices change, it is a simple process to change one number, which automatically updates the other numbers.

When the inventory is outlined in an acceptable format and you have set the ground rules for what will be counted, you are then ready to get started. Establish a basic system, count or weigh, from left to right, and top to bottom. During this process it would be wise to assign someone else to answer the phone and to take messages. Too many distractions will mean that you will never get it done. Taking inventory is an important task and should not be delegated to another employee. No one else will gain as much insight into the operation or learn more about what may be a problem than you by doing it yourself. It is your money.

Management taking inventory is hardly a waste of time; you can find treasures such as uncovered food products drying out in the back of the cooler, out-of-date stock, too much of one thing or too little of another, and food products not being rotated to ensure freshness. Of course you can also discover, in the far corner of the fridge, the growing penicillin factory. Do you think you would uncover these profit snatchers if you did not take inventory yourself? Hardly, since your underlings would likely destroy the evidence before admitting to anything.

The first few inventories you take are often the longest and most aggravating, but some minor adjustments can help you get into the right groove. Once the system is under control, it should not take long. A standard inventory taken once every month for an average-sized facility should not take more than an hour. That should be your target, and if you do not reach it within a reasonable length of time you are simply dillydallying.

One hour spent every month going through this process is worth it if helps you find out the real cost of food and supplies used for the period. Additionally, finding out what is going on, especially when it comes to the proper turnover of perishable products, is critical. You will also learn indicators that will improve purchasing practices, reduce overstocking, and minimize run-outs. Employees will be influenced by this hands-on approach to the business, as it sets the example of being willing to take the time and interest in what makes the business operate properly and according to a plan. Personal knowledge will facilitate good communication between you and your employees. You will gain more respect and lessen the chance that someone may try to cheat you.

Monthly food cost is a matter of following the established formula of opening inventory, plus purchases, minus ending inventory. If inventory has been taken consistently and purchases have been tallied so they coincide exactly with operating sales, you should be able to arrive at an accurate total cost of food used for the month. Comparing results from month to month will indicate whether you are on the right track and if it is necessary to make any adjustments. By establishing a monthly food cost, you have come a long way toward completing the monthly profit and loss statement. If you use considerable amounts of disposable items, it is important that a monthly inventory of these items be taken as well so that an accurate cost can be determined. The same goes for cleaning supplies if these are used in any significant amounts.

It is important to remember that the time taken to do an accurate and consistent inventory of consumable products at least every month will provide critical cost data information necessary from which to take corrective action. Deviations from par standards will provide clues to determine where losses may be occurring and allow you to take appropriate measures to preserve hard-earned profits. The exciting part is finding out if the operation is profitable or not. To complete a P and L report, total the cost of labor with all related taxes and fringes and include all direct expenditures for the month.

The following is a sample of a simplified P and L outline:

PROFIT & LOSS STATEMENT	
Sales for the Period	$50,000
Food Cost	
Opening Inventory	$3,000
Plus Purchases	$17,500
Total	$20,500
Less Ending Inventory	$2,500
Total Food Cost	**$18,000**
Labor Cost	

PROFIT & LOSS STATEMENT	
Management Salaries	$3,500
Hourly Wages	$11,000
FICA	$1,100
Unemployment Taxes	$400
Workers Comp	$600
Fringe Benefits	$1,200
Total Labor Cost	**$17,800**
Direct Costs	
Disposables	$2,100
Paper Supplies	$300
Cleaning Supplies	$700
Telephone	$250
Insurance	$175
Utilities	$850
Rent	$3,000
Depreciation	$1,500
Misc.	$525
Total Direct Costs	**$9,400**
Total Costs	**$45,200**
Profit (Loss)	**$4,800**

It looks and feels good to see that profit show up on the bottom line. At this point, some managers breathe a sigh of relief; others take time to congratulate themselves; and most shove the report in the file, relax a bit, and not give it a second thought. But now is the time — not just when there is a loss — when someone needs to ask some questions. Why did we do so well? Did we enjoy some unexpected sales during the period? Did we account for all the expenses accurately? Perhaps we should check our inventory counts and calculations to assure there were no errors. An overstated closing inventory left uncorrected will surely come back to bite you next period with a compensating loss. Check all cost categories to see if food, labor, and direct expenses were within budget or if one category compensated for the weakness in another. These are some basic questions that should be asked by a manager who wants to stay on top of the business. Smart managers do not take results of any kind for granted. They believe there is always something to learn from their financial reports, and there is always room for improvement.

Chapter 7

Sanitation

(You must believe.)

A food service manager's worst nightmare has to be waking up one morning and reading the newspaper headline: "Numerous customers fall ill after eating at Your Restaurant." Though no one intends for this to happen, it is a wonder that more incidents like this do not occur due to the number of food service operators who, either due to ignorance or mere inattention, disregard basic sanitation practices.

You may produce and serve wonderful food, but if you aspire to be ranked as a professional food service manager, sanitation needs to be a top priority. It is a philosophy that must start at the top of every food service organization if we are to expect cleanliness and health safety to be the universal standard for every facility that produces food for human consumption. If it is not a priority with management, the employees are not going to give it their full concern and attention either. If the public is to be guaranteed protection, the industry should insist there be strict licensing requirements for food service managers, as there are for other professionals. Why should we not expect that from the person who can put our health at risk due to a lack of knowledge or through some careless food handling act?

There are requirements in most municipalities which provide instruction and certification for managers and food service workers, but the learning time is brief. In addition, health inspectors are limited in number, and adequate enforcement in many cases is a hit-or-miss proposition. In one state, which I will leave unmentioned, a health inspector will not even come to any of the state food service facilities unless a formal complaint is registered with the department. The problem, I was told, was a severe case of lack of staffing due to underfunding by the state. Routine inspections three or four times a year will not uncover the many unsafe food-handling practices that can occur at any hour of any workday. What we have here from a practical standpoint is that public safety literally rests primarily in the hands of every individual food service manager and each food service worker. Personal responsibility, then, is the only true method that can protect the public's health, and that needs to be understood by everyone who works in the food service industry.

Certain institutions, particularly hospitals and schools, have high sanitation standards because they are carefully regulated to assure the safety and care of the public they are obligated to serve. Major companies have systems in place to inspect their operations on a systematic basis. They also recruit and train their food service managers well because they understand the importance of safe practices, and the liabilities they might encounter for causing a customer's illness can be expensive. The profit motive at work here does have some redeeming features. This factor does not guarantee full compliance in all cases, but it does improve the overall standard of safe food-handling practices.

The toughest environment to ensure proper sanitation practices in is individually owned and operated facilities. Again, it is not their intention to do the wrong thing, but for those trying hard to hold together a small business, it often does not get the priority it deserves. This is a misguided idea, since the public is sensitive about cleanliness in the places where it chooses to dine. Those operations that clearly display good practices are always in favor, which builds customer confidence and repeat business. Let us look at some of the basics on how to get this important function under control.

Communication

From the beginning, management must make the commitment to operate a business at the highest level of sanitation possible, whether it is a new startup business or when a new manager is just taking over. I have witnessed a number of brand-new food service facilities that, within a month of opening, have turned into a disastrous mess because proper cleaning practices had not been introduced at the beginning. On the other hand, I have seen a lot of older places that truly sparkle because management and the personnel care and work hard at it.

If you want to get the message across, management must clearly communicate, with the passion of a fanatic if necessary, when instructing all employees about their individual responsibility for keeping their work stations clean. Everyone needs to know up front that there is not a separate cleaning crew to clean up after everyone's messes. Besides, if employees are responsible for their own area, they tend not to dirty it up in the first place, because nobody wants to make more work for themselves. Some of the smaller restaurants let the cooks wash and sanitize their own pots. A few prima donna chefs may balk at this idea, but if the standard is set from the beginning, it will be accepted. It is surprising how many fewer pots and utensils are necessary in producing a meal after this practice is adopted. It has been an axiom in the food service industry "to clean as you go," and if the crew does that along the way, it is uncanny how little cleanup work there is at the end of a shift.

The Right Tools

Chefs are fussy about selecting the right cooking utensils, ovens, and grills to work with in the kitchen, but when it comes to the proper cleaning tools, they often are an afterthought. It does not make sense to expect having a clean operation if you do not supply employees with the proper cleaning tools. We certainly would not tolerate having dull knives and rusty pans in our food service operation, and if that were the case, any self-respecting chef would scream nasty epithets at you as he or she hastily left your employ. The workers down the chain may not be so eager to leave and may be reluctant to question why there are so few tools for cleaning. They are not going to do your thinking for you, and perhaps they just figure that's the way you want it anyway. In these circumstances you can't expect to get any higher standards than you have set for yourself.

Let us review some of the basic cleaning tools and supplies that every food service should have available in its operation:

  a. Two good straw brooms for sweeping and getting under, around, and into corners.

  b. Two dust pans strategically placed to save time walking back and forth.

  c. Two good mop handles and a case of mop head replacements. Get the medium size. The big ones are too heavy and unwieldy to handle, and the small sizes will not get the job done.

  d. Two sturdy mop buckets on wheels with a rinse attachment. A small restaurant may get by with one, but the cleaning process goes much quicker and is more effective when one bucket is used to lay down the detergent and the other is used to rinse and pick up.

e.   Several bundles of soft, absorbent rags.

f.   A plastic, one-gallon bucket for each work station. You should have at least six.

g.   A separate mop sink, which is required by law, preferably enclosed with enough room to store all cleaning equipment and supplies. This room should be organized with hanging racks and shelves so the tools and the products are handy and easy to maintain.

h.   Two to four 30-gallon trash barrels, or as many as necessary for the size of the operation, and a supply of heavy-duty plastic bags.

You should have at least two of everything because it makes sense for more than one employee to pitch in and get the job done. It is quicker, the job gets done better, and no one has to carry the entire burden. A good system, teamwork, and consistency are the key. Notice that scrub brushes were not included on the cleaning tools list; if a place requires hard scrubbing, then you have not done the necessary daily cleaning in the first place. When daily cleaning is the norm, spills do not have the time to harden, and corners do not accumulate grit. Superior results need to become a habit and a routine that is ingrained in the minds of all personnel. Staying on top with a consistent cleaning program is a lot easier than tackling a kitchen that has been long neglected. And that is when you have to go out and buy those scrub brushes.

Providing a good supply of these basic tools is a good investment that will give you the means to maintain a food service operation in first-class condition. It will pay back many-fold in much higher standards of cleanliness, because employees will have the right tools to work with. Though it may be intangible, customers will recognize it, appreciate it, and will reward it over time. In addition, having an exceptionally clean atmosphere in which to work carries over to everything else and builds a sense of pride about the workplace.

Procedures in Place and in Writing

It has been proven that people tend to believe and follow what is in print instead of what they hear. Therefore, taking the time to put cleaning procedures into written form will save much time and confusion in the end. Written procedures do not have to be fancy, and the shorter they are, the better. Be as concise as possible and do not go over one page of detailed instruction. No one has the time or desire to read that many instructions. Chances are it will be ignored.

Here is a brief sample of written sanitation instructions to all kitchen employees that can be limited to one page and can be used as a handout or as a poster.

DAILY GOOD HEALTH & CLEANING PROCEDURES

1. All food service employees will begin their shift wearing fresh, clean uniforms.

2. Employees will come to work freshly bathed, hair neatly under control, and fingernails clean and trimmed, and they will have applied deodorant.

3. All food service employees will wash their hands prior to commencing their duties, immediately after handling raw meat, and each time they use the restroom.

4. Each employee handling food will keep everything clean: hands, utensils, equipment, work surfaces, cutting boards, wipe towels, refrigerators, and sinks. Each work station shall have a one-gallon bucket filled with warm water mixed with about one measure of the prescribed sanitizer. This is to be readily available to clean and sanitize working surfaces, food processing equipment, slicers, and utensils throughout the workday. Sanitizer shall be replenished during the shift as required.

5. Keep hot foods hot and cold foods cold. The danger zone is between 40 and 140 degrees Fahrenheit; this is where bacteria can multiply rapidly.

DAILY GOOD HEALTH & CLEANING PROCEDURES

6. Do not let raw meat or poultry juices touch other foods during preparation or allow them to be stored above other foods in the refrigerator. Thoroughly wash utensils, cutting boards, and other surfaces that raw meats have touched, before reusing.

7. Mid-afternoon, between lunch and dinner and after the last dinner meal is served, the entire kitchen will be swept and mopped and all trash removed.

The seven health and sanitation standards above provide an overview of basic requirements for a typical kitchen operation. If you have special circumstances in your operation, you can tailor the information to fit your needs so the message you need to get across is clearly stated. This is a good beginning, but do not expect a written code of behavior to get the job done. A follow-up of many further details regarding safe food handling practices should be presented to all employees on a regular basis. Many managers conduct weekly employee training meetings in which sanitation topics are discussed in depth. There are also many training tools and videos available from government agencies to help you communicate important points. Also, the local health department can be called on to supply pertinent information and can be helpful in direct training. With the enormous amount of support and materials readily available, there is no excuse for any food service operation to be without an adequately trained and competent workforce.

One of the most misunderstood systems in many food service operations is the proper procedure for mopping floors. Many operators seem to think that the use of one mop and a single bucket is sufficient. This is untrue. As soon as the mop is rinsed in the bucket after the first swipe on the floor, all you are doing after that is spreading the dirt and grease around. To do it right, one must separate the process by using two mops and two buckets. The first bucket should be filled with warm water and a correct measure of floor cleaning detergent and the second bucket filled with clean rinse water. One mop generously spreads the soapy mixture on the kitchen floor and allows the detergent to work on the dirt and grime for one or two minutes. Then, follow up with another clean mop, which has been wrung out in clear water from a second bucket. Use the second mop to absorb the water and detergent that was spread on the floor by the first mop. Rinse the second mop frequently in the bucket with the clear water, and change the water as it becomes dirty. The real objective is to remove the dirt from the floor, not just spread it around. Though this procedure may sound like extra work, it only pertains to using one extra mop and bucket to get the job done. It is amazing how clean the kitchen floors will be and how quickly the task is completed, since every step in this procedure is going forward, not backward. After the job is done, be sure to discard and thoroughly rinse out the buckets and the mops in clear water, squeeze out the excess liquid, and hang them to dry.

A strong-minded dietitian introduced me to one of the most effective procedures for maintaining good sanitation and safe food handling at each workstation in the kitchen. It was the simple practice of having a gallon of warm water with sanitizer and wipe towels at each kitchen workstation for the purpose of rinsing and cleaning. These towels are a prime necessity in keeping work surfaces and equipment clean during every step of food preparation. It was a hard habit to get across to the employees, but once they were sold on the benefits, the new policy was well accepted.

Over time it developed into a good working habit, and thereby it became easier to indoctrinate new employees. The system promotes cleaning while cooking, saves time later on, and it ensures that working surfaces are constantly kept free of harmful bacteria. Additional clean towels are always available nearby for the employees to readily use. The procedure minimizes grease buildup, and it facilitates the ready cleaning of slicers, knives, and other kitchen tools used every day in food preparation. Cleaning cloths remain sanitized for the purpose intended and do not lie around getting filthy. Nothing is worse than wiping down a work surface with a greasy rag, but it happens quite often. Be exceptional and be the operator with an efficient system in place from the beginning.

Every kitchen, to be up to code, is required to have a three-compartment sink that is used to wash and sanitize all cooking utensils, knives, food containers, pots and pans, and also dishware and eating utensils, in the absence of an automatic dishwasher. The sink should be maintained and ready for use throughout the day to facilitate easy and quick washing during busy times. The first compartment is filled with hot water and detergent for washing, the second compartment filled with clear hot water for rinsing, and the final compartment with water and sanitizer. After food service items are removed from the final compartment they should then be allowed to air dry before further use. If one employee is not designated for this task, it will be up to each food service worker to wash his or her own utensils and small wares. Therefore, everyone needs to be familiar with the procedure and take responsibility for refilling the compartments whenever necessary. A sense of teamwork is required so that everyone shares fairly in this important responsibility.

The tops of counters and dining room tables, other than those covered with tablecloths, always demand special attention. Often eating utensils are directly in contact with the dining table surface, which always creates some suspicion about how clean those tabletops are. To present a good image, proper procedures need to be in place to assure customers that management is looking out for them and their safety. Have proper cleaning methods in place, such as using a sanitizer spray over the surface and then wiping dry with a clean cloth or using a clean cloth that has been immersed in a sanitizer. The key is not which method, but how it is being used. Maintaining the cleanliness of the wiping cloth is the most essential part, and this is the purpose of having the container with the sanitizer mixture close at hand. When a food service employee picks up a soiled cloth from one counter to use on another counter or tabletop without the benefit of a sanitizing rinse, correct him or her. Constant emphasis on sticking with correct procedures is a must for management.

I hope you are not having to wash all your dishware and eating utensils at a back-breaking three-compartment sink, that you have the benefit of an automatic dishwasher. However nice it is to have automation, machines can be tricky and are often cantankerous. It is best to work closely with a reliable dishwashing detergent supplier who can help keep the machine in proper working order. Suppliers are also handy in setting up proper procedures, and they may help train your employees. The main thing about automatic dishwashers is that you need to pay close attention to the correct washing temperatures, especially the 180-degree Fahrenheit final rinse temperature required for adequate sanitizing.

Inspect! Inspect! Inspect! All your planning and training efforts will be for naught if not followed through with regular inspections. The old adage, "People do what you inspect, not what you expect" has been proven true many times. It is easy to become lulled into a sense of assured expectations because you have done all the right things up to this point. Do not be the kind of manager who says, "I've told them what I want, and I certainly should expect full compliance without any further excuse." Do not leave out the most important part, which is the manager. The manager is the one who must follow through with inspections so it becomes a daily routine embedded in the psyche. Do not be a pest or obnoxious about it, but when the boss comes around and employees know he or she is serious, most will try to be on their best behavior and have good performance. If they sense a manager is not that interested, what you see may be happenstance. To expect good results, you must be sure everyone in the organization understands where you are coming from and that your expectations are not unreasonable. It should be made clear in everyone's mind that a clean and sanitary shop is paramount to preserving everyone's good health, and it is certainly a key factor to the long-term health of the business.

During my early years working as a food service manager I followed all this advice and set out to do all the things I have described so far. I set the standards, provided the training, and followed up with regular inspections. I even made a point of counseling on a one-to-one basis those employees who did not measure up. What I could not understand was why the results I was getting fell far short of what I had expected. Then I decided that perhaps I should try providing some sort of reward or some recognition for good effort that would motivate the employees to perform better. I put together a rather simple poster board display with every employee's name on it, along with columns for each week. The end of the 12 weeks just happened to be around the holidays, and the idea was that a variety of rewards could be earned through points and redeemed for prizes at the annual employee Christmas party.

Each week, I would conduct a thorough inspection of the operation and evaluate each employee's level of cleanliness at his or her workstation and assigned cleaning duties. Then, I recognized employees who had achieved a satisfactory level of performance by placing a gold star in the weekly column next to their name. Out of about 20 employees, only three earned the gold star during the first week. The following week, the number increased to five and by the sixth week, at least 85 percent were earning gold stars weekly. By that time I had raised the bar by making the standards for cleanliness a little higher.

It was simply uncanny how everyone, with rare exception, was working hard to earn that little gold star each week. The entire operation was running smoother than ever, and I found myself not having to exhort the virtues of cleanliness from my soapbox as much. That little recognition program did the job that all my lectures and cleaning lists had failed to do. At the conclusion of the program, I had arranged to recognize those employees who had earned the most gold stars over the 12-week program. I had plaques made and a modest gift presented for first, second, and third place. It was a real eye-opening experience for management to learn what it takes to motivate employees. From then on we practiced the positive and minimized the negative

There are many approaches and means to accomplishing the same goal. If you are determined not to compromise standards, then undoubtedly ideas will come. Never underestimate the wonders of the mind, and be resolute toward achieving each goal. Have confidence, and there will be a way to make it work. Management's commitment to this goal is primary, but equally so is each employee's commitment. After all the meetings and personnel training, I do not think it is asking too much to have every employee sign a pledge to practice good housekeeping and sanitation. It places the emphasis on individual responsibility, and without it, all the instruction in the world will not guarantee that the right kind of results will happen.

A pledge can be part of the hiring procedure and should be just as important as filling out the W-4 forms. Make it easy and routine. No pledge means no job. A sample pledge, including a corresponding pledge by management affirming that it is a two-way street, could be as follows:

EMPLOYEE PLEDGE

I, (Name of Employee), understand that the safety and health of our customers and employees depends mainly on the manner in which I practice proper sanitation procedures. I promise that I will learn and properly follow all food and beverage handling instructions at all times during my employment. If I have any questions or concerns about this matter, I am obligated to ask my direct supervisor.

Each job position will have different requirements, but all employees will strictly comply with the following basics:

I will initially provide my employer with a doctor's certificate saying that I am in satisfactory health to work in a food service establishment and with confirmation that I do not carry any contagious diseases.

EMPLOYEE PLEDGE

I will inform my direct supervisor about any skin cuts, open sores, respiratory colds, or coughs before reporting to work. It will not be allowed for any employee who comes in direct contact with food or beverages to return to work until all cuts and sores are completely healed and there is full recovery from any illnesses.

I will strictly follow all safety instructions regarding the handling of food and beverages at my assigned work station. I understand that the critical temperature range for the growth of dangerous food bacteria is between 40 and 140 degrees Fahrenheit. I will make every effort to minimize the amount of time that foods are allowed to remain unprotected within this critical temperature range. I will follow the procedures necessary to control safe temperatures.

Frequent and thorough hand washing with warm soap and water is required and is absolutely compulsory before returning from the rest rooms. Lack of any sanitizing products should be reported immediately.

I pledge that I understand the above basic requirements and that I will faithfully comply at all times.

Date_____ Employee Signature_____

Pledge by the Employer:

I promise to provide correct instructions on proper sanitation procedures and to supply adequate cleaning and sanitizing materials for my employees.

Date_____ Employer Signature_____

The pledge may be tougher on the management than the employee, because often, due to the demands of the business and the shortage of help, there is an inclination to overlook these strict precautions. It is a statement that requires commitment and resourcefulness, and actions in dealing correctly with this important responsibility will be a true test of professionalism. Sometimes it is harder to do the right thing, but ultimately, by maintaining the highest standards of cleanliness, customers will reward a sanitary environment with their continued patronage.

I would like to sum up this chapter on sanitation by sharing what I have come to believe are the eight major cleanliness turnoffs and what customers are silently thinking:

Streaky Silverware: This is one of the most annoying defects, especially in an upscale eatery. How managers can be unaware of this affront to the good sensibilities of their customers is beyond me, and it is so simple to fix. If you are unsure how, get some help from your detergent supplier. There are specific procedures on how to eliminate the problem permanently, and some suppliers will even offer to help train employees.

Dirty Floors: Not surprisingly, customers often look down when they are walking through an establishment, and if the floors are dirty, they become uneasy about what is in store for them. Tell personnel to keep their heads out of the clouds and look down once in a while. Please, never sweep, mop, or vacuum when customers are eating, though.

Messy Menus: Unless your place is world famous, the first impression of a dirty menu is, "What kind of a cheap joint is this anyway?"

Soiled Aprons and Uniforms: If clothes make the man or woman, think about what is being advertised by soiled aprons and uniforms. The message sent is if the service employees' attire is this dirty, just imagine what it is like on the inside of the kitchen.

The Entrance: Same as others above; the negative picture given by a dirty entrance is portrayed that much quicker. "This place must be falling fast; they can't even afford to sweep the entryway."

Condiment Containers: Not so serious, but dirty condiment containers can still be an annoyance. It takes a little more attention and work to keep them sparkling, but customers will appreciate it. It is worth the effort.

Messy and Uncleared Tabletops: "This place is not ready for me. Are they understaffed or just careless? Guess we will have to take our chances on the service here." Messy tabletops give the impression that the dining area is not clean, and this implies that the kitchen may be worse.

Sloppy-Looking Employees: "Clean maybe, but is this mess who I want serving my food? Who does the hiring around here anyway? I hope the manager's sense of style doesn't carry over into the food preparation."

Dirty Restrooms: This matter is rather self-explanatory. Nobody wants to use a restroom with no toilet paper, dirty floors, or bad lighting. Too often an empty paper towel dispenser is a real turnoff.

I am addressing the subject of sanitation with a degree of severity because, over time, I have witnessed a great many violations, most due to ignorance, lack of training, and a bad attitude. Most good operators have great intentions, but in actual practice, their behavior and performance does not always measure up to their proclamations. I believe the necessary changes will happen when people start treating sanitation with the same importance as they do employee injuries and sexual harassment violations. The health and safety of customers should never be treated with any less importance. Hitting owners and management with appropriate fines for violations will get more results than a mere warning. It would mandate training as a prime necessity and not a subject glossed over by smooth-talking managers. Most people in this business are driven by the bottom line, and that is what ultimately gets attention. Somehow, it seems to work like magic, because money is the most automatic of incentives.

Inspectors, training programs, and follow-up reviews cost money. Currently, with minimal penalties, there are few resources to attack this massive problem, and taxes are not enough to do the job right. At the time I am writing this, there are, to my knowledge, no financial penalties for food service sanitation violations. There are written warnings, required re-inspections, and the threat of closing the business, if all else fails. In rare instances, the final solution is carried out, but think about the damage that is done to the public along the way. To put some teeth into the regulations and get the owners' attention, I believe financial penalties administered for each violation would get some quick results. The fines produced would support the addition of more qualified health inspectors, help to finance the necessary means to educate food service personnel, and make food safer for the public. Justifiably, the serious violators will be stuck with the bill. A forceful program would raise the credibility of the good operators, remove the unfit, and build confidence with the public.

Restaurant associations may not agree with the financial penalties, and their members will resist any such move to legislate controls. However, if such legislation was initiated by the industry as a means to safeguard the public, it would be a significant public relations feat. Establishments that earn high marks can be properly publicized, and health safety certifications posted clearly for customers to view in all food service establishments would go a long way toward building public confidence. It is foolish to deny certification when other professions traditionally have proudly spelled it out and display it loud and clear. It is time, as an industry, that owners monitor themselves like professionals, so the public can come to regard them with the same high status.

Chapter 8

Doing the Right Things

(Do not trip over a dollar to pick up a nickel.)

Why do some managers continue doing the things that do not contribute much to the success of the business and neglect doing those things that matter? I believe it is simply human nature that draws us to do the things we already understand and know how to do well. Most of us like to operate in our comfort zone, and that means we tend to avoid the real priorities of growing a successful business.

New managers in particular face entirely new problems in areas in which they lack experience and knowledge, and it is difficult for them during the early stages of their career to decipher the priorities. As they grow in responsibility, they can become so wrapped up in the details that they sometimes miss opportunities for reaching higher ground. What they need to be doing is taking that extra step forward so they can see the view more clearly. The step required is to start doing the more important duties of management that they have not done before. Even for seasoned managers it is much easier to remain settled in a daily routine, and that way they do not have to think hard about solving the real problems. However, gravitating into a rut is a sure sign of no growth, and it is an indication that a business is not on the right track. What is of utmost importance is for management to face up to the right priorities. It is sometimes difficult to do, and it takes a certain amount of grit, but if you have the desire and passion to succeed, it will fortify your determination to get on with the business of doing the right things.

A colleague said to me, "Too often we trip over the dollars in our business to pick up nickels." What he meant was that we tend to pay more attention to the urgent rather than to what is most important. Time is wasted because some managers spend too much energy on trivial things and not enough on the things that are important in running a successful business. The more I thought about it, the more I realized he was right on target.

By illustration, he and I were visiting one of our industrial food service accounts in Nashville, Tennessee, to inspect one of our operations for quality and service. It is one of those things we believe paramount if we are to keep our clients happy, as well as making operations profitable. We first called on our client at his office to pay our respects and to inquire of his satisfaction with our company's performance. He informed us he was well pleased and expressed that he liked our manager, who he thought was a hard worker. However, he did feel the manager could use some assistance, because service occasionally suffered at peak times when the employee cafeteria was especially crowded. He did not elaborate but inferred that perhaps our company was looking more for profit gain at the expense of understaffing the food service. We, of course, expressed our concern and emphasized that our company policy was to earn our profits by serving our customers well, not by cutting corners. Sensing that it was time to stop talking and start addressing our client's concerns, we made our excuses to leave so we could examine the food operation for ourselves, since the peak of luncheon service was close at hand.

Upon entering the cafeteria, which was quite crowded with company employees, we recognized immediately what our client was saying. Some of the serving pans were less than half-full and not appealing. The server seemed to be a little rattled and unsure of the menu choices. The silverware station was in disarray and short on utensils. The paper napkin dispensers were mostly empty, and a number of them had fallen to the floor. To say the least, our food service operation was not making a good impression on our customers. Now the question was: "Where is the management?" Of all times, this should be the key time for our food service manager to be where the action was at the peak of service, but he was not to be found. Our only choice at the moment was to at least repair some of the damage.

We attempted to tidy up things at the various stations, and then one of us went into the kitchen to see if some additional food production could be expedited to replenish the serving line. Then, out of the corner of my eye, I spotted the food service manager. He was in the dish room with his sleeves rolled up working his tail off running soiled dishes through the dish machine. He had one sweaty helper with him, and the two of them were desperately trying to catch up with replacing clean service ware for the cafeteria. At first glance, it seemed rather admirable that our manager was working so hard and was willing to take over the dirty dish room job, thinking all the while how proud he was to be saving a few labor dollars.

He had a smile on his face, greeted us warmly, and he looked at us as if expecting praise for his hands-on labor. We expressed support for his efforts, but we also communicated our concern for the current level of customer service that was literally falling apart out front. He replied with some frustration that he knew things should be better, but his labor costs were getting out of line. He felt he could cover a station by himself here and there at lunch and save some operating costs. He referred to some recent memos from the home office, with the usual strong emphasis on keeping costs in line, especially labor. We both were looking at the situation from a different perspective, but for the moment, we decided to get through the lunch period as best we could before entering into a detailed discussion on how to go about resolving this problem.

One thing that I have learned over time is that it is rather futile to try to make major corrections or change someone's thinking during the heat of service. It is best to arrange a time and place when everyone can give undivided attention to the realty of what needs to be done and to give reason a chance to work. We did have an opportunity to do just that later in the day after all the serving and cleanup was done and the employees had left for the day. This gave us the opportunity to do some real problem solving in a relaxed and uninterrupted atmosphere.

Our manager was a good man and had a faithful record of service with the company. He grew up in the food service industry, was a hard worker, and had a positive attitude. This was a manager worth keeping. We just had to come to some understanding of priorities and what is meant by doing the right things. First, we wanted to hear what he thought about the problem and how it could be fixed. His reply was filled with concerns about controlling costs and the difficulty of hiring dependable help. He felt he was in a squeeze between our client, who wanted improved service, and his company's need for improved profits.

Being a loyal employee and wanting to please his employer, he decided that cutting payroll to the bone would put more money on the bottom line. Also, not replenishing the full inventory level of service ware would reduce his unit replacement costs. At least, on paper, increased profits would look good for now. For him it was still a dilemma, and the pressure was taking its toll. This is a typical situation in which a front-line manager tries to serve two masters. The situation required some deliberate problem solving, so our first approach was to put our priorities in order. We had to find a way to achieve our objective for client satisfaction and for company profits. One objective cannot stand alone without the other or else it is a bad fit for our business relationship. We all wanted a win-win situation.

After putting ourselves at ease and expressing confidence in our manager, we got down to the business of solving the problem together. We first showed why it is not a good idea for a manager to be confined to what should be a utility employee's position during peak serving times. It is obvious that this particular situation makes it nearly impossible for adequate supervision to take place. A manager has more important responsibilities, and quality customer service is the highest priority. Management needs to be free during service periods to ensure that production is being correctly paired to service requirements; that customers are being served expeditiously in a courteous manner; that service ware, napkins, and condiments are amply replenished; and that customers are being served and greeted with a smile.

Providing a friendly and pleasant atmosphere for our client's employees while serving good food is the essence of what food service management is all about. It ultimately answers the purpose of why our clients engage our services in the first place, and we cannot afford to deliver anything less. In addition, short-changing the service ware inventory exacerbates the situation even further. During the peak rush of hungry customers the available quantities of service ware were rapidly depleted, which meant someone had to constantly clean and sanitize small quantities to just barely keep up. Our initial problem was clearly defined. Next, we looked for ways to free up our manager so the duties of customer service could be attended to in the right manner.

We were not here to criticize or demean our frontline manager, but to find solutions. Before we attempted to solve the immediate issue, we thought it best to start from the beginning and determine what we were there for.

First, we made a list of our objectives, and we came to an agreement on their priorities. Number one had to be customer satisfaction. If we cannot all agree on that one, we cannot even begin to move toward a solution. Customer satisfaction should mean the same to everybody, but it is not always the case. A definition could well be: "A variety of quality food served at reasonable prices in a clean and attractive atmosphere." Read any book on the subject or pick up any magazine about the industry, and this definition is expressed in one form or another. We ordinarily accept something close to this ideal, but unfortunately solutions to real problems are not easily solved by reciting slogans. It takes a little more work than that.

The most important thing to remember is that each situation is unique, and genuine understanding comes only after a close examination of all the relative factors. Our management team, consisting of corporate, field, and front-line personnel, must meet and solve problems together and with the widest participation possible. Even though we may differ on the details of how to accomplish the number one objective of customer satisfaction, all suggestions and ideas put forth on the table should be respected and discussed. What we are looking for is the synergistic effect generated by the diverse and creative ideas put forth by all participants. When there is no such thing as rejection, people are more willing to contribute suggestions that can lead to solutions that were not even thought possible before. It takes a bit of humility on the part of the higher-ups, but if the right atmosphere is created, you will be surprised what those churning creative juices of your employees can come up with.

It is a management style that focuses more on finding solutions that will work from the ground up, rather than by proclamations from the top down. It is an attitude that communicates respect for the personnel who work every day in the trenches, a proven method that reaches out for employee participation and engages their enthusiasm and their commitment — not a bad idea for building a strong foundation for an enterprise.

If you believe customer satisfaction relates directly to sales, and more important, to repeat sales, then you have no other choice than to focus on this number one objective. It just makes sense that, without sufficient income for the business, profit objectives cannot be attained. Attentive customer service and ensuring the consistency of quality food must be primary. Food service is particularly unique in this regard, because the product and service are difficult to sustain at high levels for long periods of time. There is not much room for slack or for inattention to detail. With a brief turn of the head, an operation goes downhill fast. In addition the consumer is often compelled to choose on the basis of personal perception and mood. A bad experience mixed with a lack of attention is doomsday for the business, and that is why reaching out and giving close attention to the customer is so critical. There is a proven direct relationship between the level of customer contact and the customer's evaluation of any particular establishment. When the competition is keen, it is the edge that can make the difference between success and merely surviving.

Ensuring that the maximum number of customers are coming in the front door is the essence of doing the right thing. Spending too much time in the back of the house tending to trivial details is not where the action is. The production area needs to be under control, but that responsibility should be under the direction of the production manager or your number one cook. A small operation may not be able to afford a management-level person for that position, but at minimum, for consistent food quality, a kitchen demands the services of a highly qualified lead production person. It is difficult for any manager or owner to work in both the back and the front of the house and be truly effective in growing the business.

Here is a list of a few supporting management actions where the time spent will best achieve customer satisfaction and business success:

1. Management that knows and communicates with customers on a daily basis (this applies to the employees as well).

2. Providing a menu variety tuned to your primary customer market and promoting daily specials.

3. Carrying out an aggressive marketing and advertising program.

4. Introducing new points of service and menu promotions.

5. Quality food served at the proper temperature.

6. Recruiting and training friendly servers anxious to please.

7. Assuring clean and well-supplied service ware, trays, napkins, and condiments.

8. Keeping dining room tables and chairs cleaned and bussed promptly.

9. Providing seasonal decorations, holiday menus, and special surprise treats.

10. Presenting opportunities for customers to make suggestions for improvement.

The above list may vary from place to place, but the important thing is that the list of suggestions be developed in concert with the people most directly involved. When the manager becomes committed to these primary objectives, the next step is to get all the employees informed too. Everyone needs to understand his or her role and why it is important to give it time and attention. Managers cannot fall back and say, "Hey wait, I don't have time for all those management things when I'm occupied in the dish room." There is no way managers can get their real job accomplished if they insist on filling an employee's work station. When this realization becomes apparent, you learn a valuable lesson on what it means to be a manager. It is possible to arrive at this change in direction without lecturing if the discussion welcomes real participation and there is an atmosphere of mutual respect. It just requires the right kind of open, give-and-take communication. After all this warm and fuzzy activity, do not forget this business is to make a profit. In addition, be sure management is spending valuable time attending to these important business details:

1. Developing fairly priced menus that are attractive to customers.

2. Pre-costing recipes that will achieve the desired food cost objective.

3. Giving attention to training and keeping top-notch, reliable employees.

4. Controlling an effective purchasing program.

5. Analyzing the numbers to quickly determine and control costs.

Here again is where the manager must spend time and give his or her full energy. It does not leave much time to fill in at the dish machine station or the serving line when one of the employees has not shown up or when you deliberately under-staff to save money. It may be admirable to save costs, but this is not a good management decision.

The outcome of our problem-solving discussion in Nashville did not come easy, but it did change the direction of where and how we were going to manage at this location in the future. The focus now was on recruiting the right help and training them properly so management could be relieved to do the job it needed to do. The manager would now have the time to concentrate on management's true role of planning attractive menus, paying attention to food quality, maintaining cost controls, and, most of all, ensuring the customers were being given great service.

Managers spending their valuable time where it counts pays off in real dividends and achieving customer satisfaction at the highest level. It relates directly to a client's appreciation of our services. When the food service is excellent, you can negotiate on firm ground when you need better contract terms. When inflation takes its toll, a highly satisfied client is much more willing to cooperate in helping us to reach our financial goals because he wants to keep us on the job and to continue doing well. A high level of customer satisfaction also relates directly to higher participation and improved revenue. If price increases are a definite necessity, they risk being more acceptable to customers when they are accompanied by value, quality, and good service.

Everyone comes out a winner. Put that strategy against saving a few dollars by cutting corners that result in poor service and lower sales, and the math does not add up. The business priority of a food service manager must be top line and customer driven. Do not be guilty of tripping over a dollar to pick up a nickel.

Chapter 9

The Greeter

(Sieze the moment.)

Have you ever entered a restaurant anticipating an enjoyable experience, and for some unknown reason there is no one there to greet you? It is a disappointment, and it registers an immediate negative message in your mind. You expected at least a bit of friendly recognition since you chose to spend some of your hard-earned money at this restaurant. You might even wonder what you are doing there. Perhaps, if managers played the customers' role and came through the entrance of their establishments on occasion, they would learn something about the impressions made by their employees at that first, fundamental contact. First impressions can literally make or break you in this business, and you usually do not have more than ten seconds to make the right one. That first greeting customers receive is the beginning of their dining experience. It is the basis of what we all yearn for — some bit of recognition that we as individuals are important.

People cannot stand to be ignored or, even worse, be given one of those I-could-care-less that-you-are-here welcomes. The good food an establishment is known for is not the only thing that draws customers. They also come to enjoy the total experience, to be comfortable, to feel good. The attitude of the greeter sets the stage and can determine the diner's level of pleasure with the total meal service.

The choice of where people decide to eat out often rests on an emotional decision, not just convenience, or even price. People remember and appreciate the small pleasantries, and it begins with how they are greeted at an establishment. Creating good memories for customers helps build repeat business, which is absolutely essential if you want to be successful long term. This is a philosophy that needs to be impressed upon the minds of all employees. Of course, it has to begin with a positive management policy about making first impressions, and it has to be firmly implemented as standard procedure.

Management has to believe in the importance of making that first good impression with every customer, new and old. The effort makes it known that the establishment does not take people and their business for granted. Selecting the right person for the job as front of the house greeter is a critical decision for management. It is not something that should be done capriciously, but done with the utmost of care, because who is chosen is, in essence, your personal representative. A greeter should have the ability to greet customers with a genuine smile, give direct eye contact, along with body language that unmistakably communicates, "I'm glad to see you." It is possible to train someone to be outgoing with a smile, but it is a lot easier to invest in someone who is naturally endowed with the right personality for the job in the first place. There may not be time to play the part of *My Fair Lady*'s Professor Higgins.

Many food service establishments place someone in this position who may be attractive and have a pleasant personality but usually has little experience or authority.

I believe, for the benefit of a business, someone at the supervisory level who has the experience and the skill to run the entire front of the house is best to promote customer service, assign seating, and train and supervise the service staff. A good choice would be an accomplished waitperson or a server with high ambitions and a potential for leadership. Someone whom others perceive as outgoing and who has a natural gift for relating well to people is good. Because this is a key position and it is vital to the success of a business, it is imperative to make this choice with great care. The time taken to make the right investment here will pay handsome dividends.

The greeter is the person most responsible for customer relations but can have any title that seems appropriate. It could be the assistant manager, head waiter or waitress, dining room supervisor, host or hostess, or head server in the cafeteria. The person selected is important, but just as much so is a description of the position with a list of clearly stated responsibilities and authority. The following is a sample guide for a dining room supervisor's position in a typical restaurant:

Position: Dining Room Supervisor

Objective: To assure that every customer is greeted and served with the utmost friendliness, courtesy, and efficiency. Leads and trains the dining room staff to perform their customer service duties with pride and excellence.

RESPONSIBILITIES AND AUTHORITY

- Responsible for the proper arrangement and setup of tables and chairs before the dining room opens.

- Ensures there is an adequate supply of clean service ware, utensils, and napkins available and ready. Assigns and directs all side duties of the wait staff.

- Reviews the menu and the time requirements for the preparation of various items on the menu prior to opening.

- Responsible for the deportment of the wait staff on the floor. Keeps everyone attentive to their duties and to their assigned guests.

- Is fully prepared to open the dining services on time and is ready to greet incoming guests in a warm and friendly fashion.

- May also be in charge of bar service (depending on the management structure of the business).

Note the emphasis on being prepared and communicating with the service employees prior to every meal service. That means every day, not just on occasion when something new needs to be addressed. Consider it as a drill before every opening by getting everyone's attention and priming everyone's attitude focused in the right direction. Treat it like show business, and make every meal service a new opening. Most of all, management needs to get excited, too. This is a great business; it should be fun, and a healthy charge of adrenaline can help motivate. Do not think this is silly and start taking the outset of every meal service as just routine. When that happens, a little dullness starts to creep in, and the service begins to lose some of the crispness the establishment has worked so hard to attain. When the business first started everyone was excited, and there were many training meetings that were much like pep rallies. Some of that same spirit needs to continue to maintain quality and keep improving. Doing it well is a matter of personal discipline that requires strength of purpose and a strong desire for excellence. It is never taking service standards for granted that distinguishes those businesses that far outshine the competition over time.

The greeter, if not in uniform, should be dressed fashionably but not overdressed for the type of food service image desired. Neatness, alertness, poise, a genuine smile, and the giving of a cordial greeting are the primary prerequisites. Remembering names is a real plus, and keeping a card index of regular customers on file can be helpful. This is a worthwhile task, so help the greeter set this up as a standard procedure. It is a challenge for any greeter to accomplish, and those who do it well are recognized as exceptional. Customers will love it, and the only problem that may arise is keeping the greeter from being hired away. These positions have high visibility, so be aware that good recruiters are always on the alert for people with this special talent, especially those who carry it off with a dynamic personality. Do not worry, however, as long as employees are well-rewarded and appreciated.

The greeter, in essence, is the frontline manager, supervisor, or whatever level of responsibility is deemed appropriate for the type of food service operation. This is the first impression, and it is important to assign the best person possible to this position. A proficient greeter knows the food service operation in every detail and displays a high degree of confidence. Customers easily recognize demeanor of this kind when they are first greeted and get a good feeling that they are going to be well served. The greeter knows what tables are available without having to ask the guest to wait. When extra setups and chairs are needed, they are taken care of before escorting the guests to their table. Unneeded setups are removed from the table, and in some instances, extra chairs. Do not forget to make special accommodations if children are in the party, and do a little extra to recognize and make them feel welcome. Parents who are naturally under a certain amount of stress will greatly appreciate the thoughtfulness and will likely remember it well when it comes time to choose their next outing.

When everything is prepared for seating and there has been a wait, another greeting and warm smile is in order. It shows customer appreciation for any delays and helps to build their spirits in anticipation of an enjoyable meal. The greeter then shows the guests to their table saying, "This way please," and leads them carefully but not too fast so they will not get lost in the traffic. If possible, seat women guests so they face the dining room instead of the wall. One restaurateur once observed, "When you seat a woman dining with her male companion so that she faces the wall, the chances are ten to one she will pick a quarrel with him before the dessert is served."

After the guests are seated, hand them menus, and for couples, begin with the lady. After seating a large party, begin with the person to the right of the host and proceed counterclockwise around the table. The host may indicate as soon as his party has been seated that he will order for the entire group. If menus have already been distributed, collect only those handed back voluntarily. When there is not a children's menu available, it is not advisable to give regular menus to small children unless the parents request it.

The greeter's job should not be limited to the task of the initial greeting and the seating of customers in the dining room. The responsibility should go further by continuously checking on whether any guests in the dining area are in need of service. An experienced greeter is sensitive to "searching looks" in the dining room and does not wait around for problems to arise, but is the one who initiates inquiries of needed assistance. The response to customer needs can be done, or the appropriate waitperson can be directed to handle the request. In passing tables en route after seating guests, every opportunity should be taken to inquire of other guests, "How is everything?" The approach taken by the best establishments is to train their personnel to treat customers as if they were guests in the employees' own home. It is not a bad mind-set; it helps in developing a healthy service attitude, and it makes the job more enjoyable for everyone. The greeter's position in a popular restaurant is for someone who thrives on keeping busy and has the capacity to stay on his or her toes at all times. Someone with the attributes of personal enthusiasm, a high degree of people skills, and who takes a great deal of pride in food service is fit for this position.

Saying, "Goodbye, I hope you enjoyed your lunch or dinner," to departing guests is just as important as greeting them when they first entered the establishment. The greeter then has an opportunity to learn whether the guests enjoyed the meal and the service or if some misunderstanding arose. Any required adjustments should be made immediately. Good will is engendered when explanations, not excuses, are provided. The reason most customers do not return if they are displeased with something is because their problem was not recognized or corrected in a timely manner, and the chance of retaining their business is not likely to come again.

Try to read between the lines if their response to the inquiry is lukewarm or just a passing, "It was all right." An experienced greeter is sensitive to these signals, because they know most people do not like to complain. Making amends at the time takes someone quick on his or her feet and truly determined to make every customer satisfied. Responses will depend on the circumstances but at the minimum should at least entail an apology. Crediting part or all of the meal or a gift certificate are possible ways that can effectively diffuse the disappointment if presented with sincerity. A follow-up call with an added incentive can often make a friend for life. It takes extra effort to make the call, and it costs a little at first, but it gets results. It is amazing how few food service establishments will make the effort. Those that do consider it a good investment are greatly rewarded.

Business cards are not just for the owner or the manager, but for everyone on the wait staff. They are not that expensive, and they add class. If you are worried over wasting money and cards, perhaps have a waiting period for new hires until they succeed through their initial trial period. Turnover may cease to be such a big problem when wait staff employees take pride in having their own business cards. This can be just one of the little things that help to build self-esteem and loyalty to the employer. The reason to invest in a business is to make a return on that investment. A fifteen-dollar investment in the employee to help build customer contacts may be a good return. I remember well that the most popular of all establishments that I had ever worked in made sure all their key wait staff, bartenders, and managers had personal business cards from day one. Make the investment if it is a good fit for your type of business.

Name tags are important too. Do it right and get some decent looking ones. This is another opportunity to present the staff in a classy way and to build pride in people. The purpose is to provide individual recognition and is helpful in making a new employee feel welcome. It is a way for everyone to get to know each other's names, and it helps to foster cooperation and teamwork. Customers especially like it since they can call out a name for service instead of, "Hey, waiter, I need my check."

Greeters are not necessarily only in the domain of fine dining establishments. Whatever the level of food service, the principle is the same. The main idea is to let people know they are welcome. It is that simple, and this manner of service does not necessarily require additional staff or expense. The role of the greeter can be performed by anyone in the establishment who first encounters an entering customer. It could be the counter server, cashier, waitperson, busboy or busgirl, or the employee who may be preparing the order directly at point-of-service establishments. It is not an exclusive assignment by any means. The point is that most people like to be recognized, preferably with a person's full attention and sincerity. It clearly proclaims you are glad to see them, paying attention, and ready to be of service.

Over the years, I have had the pleasure of working with countless individuals who have served and performed as great greeters. Two employees that I most remember for their outstanding ability to charm customers were Carl, the chef-manager at the Rathskeller at Cornell University, and James, the head server at the American Café at the University of Houston. What I remember most was that both greeted customers with a great smile, along with a genuine and friendly salutation. How they kept it up with such consistency I will never know, but it was catching. Other employees began imitating them. Even when they had personal problems and difficulties to deal with, they seemed to have the special ability to tune it out and to turn on their smiles for the customers. They knew intuitively that customers were special and that their number one job was to please. They enjoyed serving people, and it showed. Neither, as far as I know, was trained that way, at least not by management; it was just the way they were. These folks made the operation click, and they certainly made management look good. I still wonder if management ever appreciated or even understood their true worth. However, to their credit, they were often recognized by customers and on occasion were suitably acclaimed with a complimentary campus news article. It seems, to be a success in this business, you need to search for these exceptional individuals, and once found, give them some leeway and a good reason to stay.

Never be too busy to make the effort to greet customers with great enthusiasm. Even during those peak times when things are hectic, there has to be someone to at least recognize the customer in a friendly manner. When chaos reigns, and it will at times, it does not take much for at least one of the employees near the front to take a moment to explain that someone will be at their service shortly. It is that bit of reassurance that the customer is not being ignored, and the gesture proclaims that your establishment appreciates their business. That first impression sets the stage for an enjoyable experience, the kind that keeps drawing your customers back time and time again. Doing it every day and keeping all employees primed with the same attitude should be one of the most fundamental responsibilities of every good manager.

Chapter 10

Employee Communication

("Please tell me what you want.")

Few food service companies today can claim that they have easy-to-understand job descriptions for their employees. Correct procedures on what to do and how to do it are deemed important because, if strictly followed, they are expected to achieve desired results. However, it is the desired goal that is usually missing, specifically a clear description of what result, behavior, or service is expected. Often, this message is entangled in the procedures and does not get to the essence of what it is we are trying to accomplish. This is because written job descriptions often emphasize "how to" procedures with little detail on the results that are expected. It is a matter of explaining to employees in understandable language what exactly you want from them.

Job descriptions that outline expected results in writing are useful, but without some verbal explanation, along with some enthusiastic body language, the written communication by itself does not make much of an impression. The employee wants real meaning to the message, and a little verbal fire on the part of the instructor helps to expound what is expected. The worst thing to do to a new employee is to ignore him or her. Wake up, management; this is a living asset, a personal representative, the person who is going to present a direct service to the customer. Take the time and pay attention to this new employee up front, when fresh eyes and ears are more receptive to orientation and training. Trying to correct performance errors later on is time consuming and expensive, and the worst scenario is losing a potentially super employee because of management neglect. Spend time where it counts. Developing high employee performance from day one is what smart managers consider a good investment.

To communicate clearly what is expected from employees, begin by saying, "An excellent result is when," and then describe in detail what that means. Instead of labeling these job descriptions, call them "performance objectives." The following are a few examples of communicating performance objectives for some basic food service positions:

Dish Room/Sanitation Performance Objectives

An excellent result is when...

1. All service ware (glasses, utensils, dishes, and food containers) are returned for service spotlessly clean, sanitized, and streak free for use by customers.

2. Cleaning materials and chemicals are measured and used in the correct amounts.

3. All cleaning tools, such as mops and brooms, are handled with care, thoroughly cleaned, and returned to their proper storage area after each use.

4. Machinery and equipment are operated according to instructions and maintained in a clean and sanitary condition.

5 Work is accomplished in cooperation and in harmony with fellow employees.

Hot Food Preparation Performance Objectives

An excellent result is when...

1. All menu items are prepared by recipe and all ingredients are measured accurately.

2. Hot food is prepared progressively throughout the meal service period to ensure that food items are served at their peak quality.

3. Correct cooking temperatures are followed to obtain maximum yields and optimum taste.

4. All food is served at its proper temperature.

5. Fresh and attractive garnishes are used to complement serving plates, platters, or pans.

6. Cleaning of utensils, equipment, and working surfaces is accomplished throughout the preparation.

7. High standards of personal hygiene and appearance are maintained.

8. All cooked and uncooked food not currently being used for production or service is properly covered and returned promptly to refrigeration.

9. Attitudes are friendly and cooperative with all people.

10. An interest is taken in customer satisfaction and suggestions for improvement are made voluntarily.

Food Server Performance Objectives

An excellent result is when...

1. You know the menu well and the key ingredients and are able to assist customers in making choices by making suggestions.

2. You give every customer that you serve the best smile, good eye contact, and full attention.

3. You are alert and quick without giving the appearance of being hurried.

4. You pay close attention to the appearance of the food being served to ensure it is appealing to the eye and served at the proper temperature.

5. You are helpful to others and give full cooperation to fellow workers and management.

Written performance objectives should be concise, limited to a single page, and in plain, easy-to-understand language. Tailor the most preferred objectives for almost any job with a brief statement following the words, "An excellent result is when." Of course, time and attention must be applied to the "how to" training as well, but it is the results of that training that is the ultimate objective. Clarity is of utmost importance so results are easy to observe and measure. Excellent job performance is what managers should expect from their employees, but unless there is some degree of personal interaction between management and employees on a regular basis, these objectives are hard to achieve. They should not be left to chance by handing out a few written objectives to an employee without personal coaching and expecting automatic high performance. The importance of training cannot be left to chance. Management must take the time and believe in the high standards it is trying to communicate for employees to accept these goals as their own. Unless there is some personal involvement taken by management, written performance objectives do not always produce exactly what is expected.

Food service companies spend a lot of money researching and producing some excellent training materials, but they need to be put to good use or they all go to waste. Too often the training manuals, with all their detailed procedures and good advice for accomplishing numerous food service tasks, wind up collecting dust on bookshelves behind the manager's desk. Perhaps there is too much material, too much intricate detail applicable only in certain situations, too much of it out of date, or never enough time on the front lines to implement it. There is always some excuse why training is given the short end, and often it is simply due to the urgency of just keeping up with the day-to-day business. There never seems to be enough time to get around to training. The pressure to make higher profits keeps management ranks thin and limits the availability of support staff. There is only so much time and energy to go around, so when it comes to training, all agree it is a good idea and keep promising themselves that when things ease up a bit, they will give it some attention. If this problem persists in an organization, it means priorities are mixed up. It does not make sense trying hard to get results when all you have to work with is an untrained and unmotivated staff. Short-circuiting the development of personnel can lead to the early demise of a business. It is a matter of management putting first things first.

Many of the smaller food service operators and the independent restaurants do not have the resources, the time, or the money to develop comprehensive job training manuals. Here again, the desired results left to chance can quickly lead to disaster. Having great employees is a help, but do not count on always being lucky. There must be a better way, and I suggest keeping it simple. This is not a complicated business when it comes to the many tasks that must be accomplished. However, those tasks must be done well.

You must depend on employees to achieve the necessary results, but they have to understand what is expected. In other words, they need to know clearly what to do but not every detail on how to do it. That is not to minimize the importance of procedures that are clearly written, but by themselves, they are incomplete. The critical aspect is the final result. For example, if the dishwasher does everything according to his job description and still comes up with a few dishes with specks of dried food residue, this is not a satisfactory result. What then happens is that a customer may reach for a plate at the salad bar and become rather annoyed. Service ware that was wet or streaky, had dried soap residue, and was not as sparkling clean as it should be might be reset at a table. It gives further doubts about the sanitation and even about the food being ordered. This is not what to expect from a well-managed restaurant. People will remember this poor standard and quite likely never return.

An employee, such as a dishwasher, may be following job procedures exactly — pre-rinse, proper temperature, correct amount of detergent, and the final rinse — but there is one critical step missing: employees need to inspect and return to service every dish and utensil sanitized and cleaned for use by the restaurant's customers. When washing thousands of service ware by either hand or machine, it is possible that a few will not get perfectly clean. However, a good dishwasher with the right attitude and a good eye can keep mistakes to a minimum. Foremost, the employee must have an understanding that it is his or her job to always provide perfectly clean service ware for the customer, and a good dishwasher with a sense of responsibility will take on the job of inspecting his own work. The real difference is in producing the desired results, not just making a good effort. You should continue following correct procedures and the proper steps to accomplish a given task, but it is the extra attention to detail that gets the job done perfectly every time.

In communicating what results are expected from employees, the two key ingredients are to define exactly what results are expected and the type of attitude every employee must bring to the job. It is not something that can be forced. It must be a voluntary action coming from a sense of personal responsibility. Some say this is impossible, that you cannot convert people to your way of thinking or try to instill hourly employees with the same sense of dedication thought reserved only for managers and owners. Some do not believe that employees are capable of having a deep sense of personal pride in their work. This hard-line type of owner or manager usually organizes the business with tight controls and stiff penalties for substandard work. Supervision is strong and prevailing. Turnover is high, and more time and expense becomes necessary to recruit constant replacements. Attitudes are usually negative toward the workforce, and desired results are forced at best. This kind of working environment breeds mistrust and creates a fertile breeding ground for union organization.

By contrast, look at a management style that believes all people have value and, if given the chance, want to work and do a good job. A positive outlook toward the workforce allows people to perform at their best. From the beginning, the right attitude about employees and an understanding of human motivation must start at the top.

The main thing for managers to understand is that they are not dealing with machinery, and they must know how to deal with different types of people, which is more complicated. This is a people business, and as long as food preparation, service, and cleanliness are the principal functions, it will always remain a people business. The job is important, and you must rely on individuals to get the job done right. Therefore, it makes sense that if you expect good results, you first must treat the employee as the most important component of the business. If not just for altruistic reasons, do so for selfish ones because, in reality, it directly relates to success and profitability.

Again, it begins with management's attitude and a willingness to take the time to treat employees well and communicate with them in a positive manner so that each employee knows he or she is important. It is simple to do. Treat employees on an individual basis the same way you would treat any important person. Give good eye contact, express sincerity, appreciation, and individual attention. Add a little patience for those who need extra time and training, and wonders will happen in the operation. Some say that may be nice in theory, but in the real world people are not like that. Almost every food service manager I have ever known has at least once remarked that his or her biggest problem was getting good help. At a higher level, the biggest problem always seemed to be getting good managers who knew how to train and motivate employees. This sounds like the chicken or the egg dilemma: which comes first, good employees or good managers. The answer can be related to sports when looking at the extraordinary effort going into recruiting top-quality coaches for various professional and amateur teams. It appears the wisdom is in getting the right leadership first; the right players will follow. The level of performance rises dramatically for the team's players when their natural talents are developed under a great coach.

In my experience, I have seen many good employees run off by poor managers, and on the other hand, many good employees who have made poor managers look good. Again, the responsibility starts at the top. To begin with, an employee has to be instilled with a sense of purpose that is a lot larger than just the job that they were hired to do. The best time to do this is when you have every individual's attention. This has to be when a new employee is hired or closely after a new manager arrives on the scene.

It is the window of opportunity when people are most attentive and willing to listen to what is expected.

It starts with communicating a mission statement, which is a declaration of the purpose and desired result. Making a lot of money may have been the initial motivation, but for this purpose, project the mission on a higher plane. Making a simple statement that indicates aspirations to be the finest establishment of its kind with a reputation for serving excellent food and providing extraordinary service is a good beginning. Continuing in that vein, to reach this lofty goal, employ a team of employees who have a sense of personal pride and a caring attitude to perform at their best. Above all, commit the owner and the managers of the enterprise to apply their experience and knowledge in a manner that assists every individual in their employ to reach their greatest potential. Affirm that mutual respect between management, employees, and all individuals will be standard conduct.

These are some managers that can instill the idea that there is a mission worth undertaking. It is a stated goal that you aspire to and follow by describing the precise manner in which you intend to reach that goal. Formulate this concept with original ideas so the message comes across as sincere. It has to be authentic to be accepted in the minds of the people needing motivation. An individual and a company with a great idea must understand that higher goals can be attained only by having a cast of employees who are willing to follow the lead. It is when employees wholeheartedly buy in to what the business is trying to achieve that you can claim credit for being a good leader.

Clarify objectives in writing before getting over-involved with developing detailed job descriptions on how to do everything. Employees with the right objective in mind and a good attitude will often come up with a better way to do it anyway. Just tell them what is expected. The results will tell whether or not you are managing.

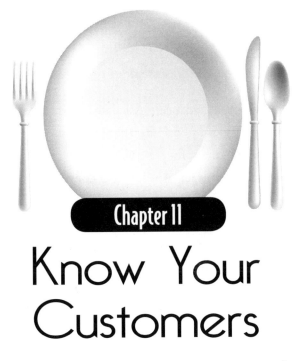

Chapter 11

Know Your Customers

(How to develop and nurture the most important component of your business.)

There are many reasons put forth as to what determines the lack of growth or the ultimate failure of a food service business. Insufficient sales, poor management, location, high rents, and under capitalization are a few of the valid causes that can contribute to the final outcome. These are the usual and the rational reasons, but sometimes they do not reveal the whole story. There are intangibles at work in every business, often unnoticed, and food service operations have more than their fair share. When the competition is keen and companies vie with each other for a better share in the marketplace, it is essential to have an edge. If you are seeking an advantage, one of the most important factors in successfully securing and keeping business is to develop a variety of personal relationships with customers. Some may consider this unnecessary, believing that providing good food and good service is sufficient. Others who are interested in developing better customer relations would like to try, but for one reason or another, something else diverts and consumes their time and attention. Perhaps it is a matter of choosing priorities. Truly appreciating the importance of customer relations and how it affects business can motivate a manager to find the time.

For a number of years, I had been associated with a major food service management company that was in the business of contracting with institutions to operate their food services. One of our company's best university food service contracts was lost to a competitor after several years of what we had thought was a good relationship. As was the practice at the time, one of our top executives went to visit the president of the institution after the cancellation of our contract to inquire of the unforeseen reason for our termination. This loss caught us all by surprise, for we had received little criticism about the food or the service over time. What we were told at the "post-mortem" was also a surprise, and for us it turned out to be a wake-up call.

The reason for their change was not due to food quality, service, or price, but something that had bothered them for some time. It was simply that they seldom saw or had any kind of a relationship with our local manager. The food service was good, there was little to complain about, but the manager always seemed to be in his office and obviously busy at work. Nothing would have changed except our competitor came along with a better idea. It brought along a manager candidate who was personable and expressed a strong desire to work closely with the students and the staff to improve the food service program. The personal energy the manager displayed and his enthusiasm about special events and innovations convinced our client that it was time for a change.

We were simply outsold, and it had nothing to do with price. It meant more to our client, especially with an audience confined to living in its "second home" to have a restaurant managed by a person who was a good communicator and willing to get involved with campus life. It was then the light went on, and the strategy for our entire company completely changed. We came to realize that active and open relationships with our customers were a crucial key to retaining business. It was not a substitute for good performance, which is a given, but it came to be an essential requirement if we were to successfully maintain long-term relationships with our clients.

Shortly thereafter, managers in the field began receiving memos from the regional office with an ink stamp affixed to the bottom, labeled "90/10." No one seemed to understand what this meant, and we thought perhaps it was some kind of office code that did not concern us. That was soon to be corrected at the forthcoming managers seminar, which was soon to take place. It was at that meeting that our regional executive related the story about the lost account and the reasons why. He also expressed disappointment that no one had inquired about the 90/10 stamp that had recently gone out to all the managers in several communiqués. We found out about it pretty fast. 90/10, we were told, was the new policy being instituted for all unit managers in the field. It meant we should spend 90 percent of time with customers and 10 percent of time in so-called administrative duties.

For those of us who got the message and gave it our best shot, it did work. We had to change the way we managed, we had to delegate more of the minutia, and we had it set in our minds that good customer relations was job number one. With some added imagination, managers started building upon the idea and came up with all kinds of ways to relate better and make the food service more fun. Managers began overcoming their shyness and started spending more time in the dining room in contact with their student customers. Overall communication was not necessarily about food quality but tended to be more about campus activities, politics, and the outcome of the previous night's basketball game. Managers learned to become more social, and students realized that managers were becoming more approachable and willing to listen to their concerns. It was a new discovery that people and their personalities did make a difference in the perception of the food service program. This was the beginning of a new era that significantly changed our company's style of management for the better.

New ways were promoted to make food services fun, and the concept of monotony-breakers and special events became standard fare at all our accounts. Awards were given out to those who came up with the best ideas. Best of all, our customers joined in and helped create and participate in some special events. Many enjoyed dressing up for the various themes and often supplied the musical talent for everybody's enjoyment. It was party time facilitated by management, who opened the doors and made it possible. All it took was coordinating a plan and a theme through the efforts of a joint customer and management committee to develop the appropriate menu, add a few decorations, some music, and a little publicity, and the event was ready to go. This was a lot more imaginative and exciting than just serving pumpkin pie at Thanksgiving.

Each year, as part of the usual forecasted budget plan, it was required for managers to come up with their annual calendar of special events. Those who were not as creative as others were given ample support to ensure every food service operation had a plan and had the capability and the resources to deliver it. When these activities are well done, one of the side benefits is that communication with customers is immensely improved, and the overall perception of the dining services is elevated to a positive level of enjoyment, rather than a subject of criticism. In this new atmosphere, it becomes evident when inquiring about the quality level of the food services the responses from students usually depend on the variety of special events that are presented over the course of the year. The positive aspects of a fun-filled program make those inevitable burnt toast errors seem less significant.

When customers are part of a residential setting, such as dormitory students, the elderly in retirement homes, and even the military, the food services they are obliged to attend can soon become repetitious and boring. It takes a creative food service manager to make three meals a day, seven days a week interesting. There are only so many ways to serve hamburger, and though hard to admit, some people even enjoy a change from mother's cooking. When in the military, I was, like most servicemen, frequently transferred from one installation to another. During the first couple of months at each location, I thought the food served was good, but soon after that it seemed to go downhill fast.

Evidence of this same type of experience comes about every year at university food services, especially during the early part of November, when student complaints about food services take a dramatic rise. Of course, about that time, mid-term exams contribute a certain amount of student tension, which does not help the situation. If something new and interesting is not planned in the dining service program, you can almost set the clock on the time when trouble begins to start. The calendar of special events certainly helps to moderate some of the problems, but the Halloween pumpkin-carving contest alone does not do the job. This is where a plan of weekly events, though perhaps not as elaborate, can be implemented to provide some change to the normal routine. These zestful surprises came to be known as monotony-breakers. The idea was to keep the "captured audience" in suspense, wondering what those crazy people in the dining hall were going to come up with next. It helps to be a bit crazy in this business. Some of the most popular were build-your-own sundaes, candlelight with strolling guitars, clowns handing out candy bars, wild costume contests, a surprise Dixieland marching band, big-screen cartoons, local guest chef, and barbecue cookouts.

The ideas are limited only by your imagination, so let them fly free. If you are stumped in coming up with something new to do, there are plenty of fresh ideas available if you talk to students or your employees. Having more people involved produces that much more fun and participation in the dining hall. Keep the program interesting, and there is not much time left to complain. It is amazing what a different attitude customers start to have toward "their food services." Unless you are a die-hard office jockey, it is impossible not to have numerous opportunities to interact and get to know the people being served.

The best part is good customer relations are being built on a positive plane, rather than on an adversarial one. It is the age-old strategy of a good offense beating a good defense, and it changes the entire atmosphere from negative to positive. Of course, it does not eliminate a certain amount of complaints, which should be received and acted upon with all seriousness, but the relationship functions on a more cooperative and friendly basis. The food service manager now fits more in the category of one of the good guys, rather than a constant object of criticism. He or she becomes easier to approach, and the growing mutual good will encourages the management to further seek out and get to know customers better. They no longer need to be strangers.

An excellent time to start making friends out of strangers is on new beginnings. There is no better time to meet and greet than when a new school semester commences or when new residents arrive for the first time at their retirement home. Break the ice by conducting an open house, reception, or any scheme devisable to bring people together. Everyone is usually a little nervous about new surroundings, and most need a little encouragement to start conversing with people they do not know. This is an opportunity to meet the manager and learn that there is a real person in charge who is interested in customers' welfare.

This is important since, in today's world, people's opinions of administrators, city hall, or whatever the hierarchy, is that those people seem to care more about their own status than they do about the individual. Right or wrong, it is a jaded point of view created over time, maybe due to some frustrating personal experiences, which need to be turned around. The initiative to change this attitude needs to be taken by the management in charge if a good working relationship is to start out right. Do not forego this opportunity to get acquainted early on.

The food service department does not necessarily have to go down this road alone. It is a good idea to collaborate with the administrators of the institution, who in many cases, also need a nudge to get out there and press the flesh. Besides, you might be able to convince them to share some of the expenses involved in creating special events. A reception does not have to be a huge, expensive affair, but it is important to produce an atmosphere in which it is comfortable for people to mix and meet one another. The food can be relatively simple, such as a variety of cookies, tea sandwiches, and some punch.

Depending on the circumstances, alcoholic beverages can loosen up the occasion a bit, but only if appropriate. The presentation is what is important. A nicely decorated food and beverage table on display with colorful napkins and a flower arrangement can look quite elegant at little cost. I have always thought some light background music added style and helped put people in a good mood. Here again, it can just as easily be taped music or, if affordable, a live trio. Whatever is done, the main idea is to indicate that you are glad to meet the newcomers and to open the door for some friendly getting-to-know-you conversation.

Depending on the weather or the time of year, an event that is staged outdoors, such as a picnic lunch or even just an ice cream social, is a way to bring strangers together and to have some fun. Since this is the beginning of a relationship, having newcomers can be advantageous because they have nothing to complain about. Do not be too relieved yet, for the next move is to have another of these gatherings in three to four weeks. Do not wait too long, for then you will be encountering the more serious concerns that have had time to fester. This secondary get-together is the time to be a good listener. It is a reality check to determine if you are on the right track and to give ample time to make corrections. The attack method of managing a food service delivery system is to always be one step ahead of any impending crisis. Waiting around for complaints to start coming presents a defensive posture and does not help credibility. By taking the initiative, it displays a willingness to admit that you are not all that perfect and that you care about making things right.

Another excellent tool in maintaining good communication with in-house residents is a well-functioning food service committee. It works best when the board is composed of members from a broad cross-section of the resident population. Ideally, on a campus it would be participants from every class level and from each of the individual colleges on campus. On rather large university campuses, to be more applicable, each food service location would in addition have representation from its own local committee. Residents in a retirement home should also strive for some degree of representation.

What should be avoided is a group of individuals who act more like a clique and who are just there to advance their own personal agendas. Meetings should be held on a regular basis with a specific agenda to follow so that common concerns can be addressed. Unless there are critical issues pending, meetings every week tend to become repetitive and a little boring, causing attendance to suffer. Bi-weekly seems to be an ideal period of frequency, which allows enough time for certain recommended actions from previous meetings to have made some progress and perhaps even been accomplished. A sense of formality should be established, along with appropriate standards of protocol, to give the group a sense of status. The keeping and the review of minutes is important so everyone is clear on what concerns need to be addressed and how they are to be resolved. The committee can be made up of volunteers who have a sincere interest in helping to make the food service program better, or depending on the political environment, their peers from various sectors of the institution can nominate individuals. In any case, the committee should be representative of the entire body of participants who use the food services and should take the responsibility seriously. It is also their duty to communicate their activities back to the body about how specific concerns have been resolved and to continue soliciting further ideas for improvement. On occasion, it is a good move to invite non-members to the food committee meetings to introduce a new voice and to present a different slant on what people are thinking. A well-functioning food committee is a good communications tool, and if used effectively by management, permits a wonderful opportunity to get to know a variety of customers on a personal basis. Something positive happens to strengthen the relationship when problems are addressed and common solutions come about. It then becomes a team effort, working together rather than an adversarial relationship in which the only thing that seems to come about is the drafting of a long list of grievances. Things do not get done, and people do not get along when working in an atmosphere of constant criticism. However, it is management's role to initiate the program, set the stage, organize the players, and be willing to take some heat. When customers know that someone listens and then does something about solving their problems, they will begin working with management as partners, not as adversaries.

Food committee members are usually the outgoing kind and enjoy the social interaction, but what about the loners? These independent types do not have any interest in participating in formal groups. They are prevalent in every residential setting, and it takes a little extra maneuvering on the part of management if they are to be reached. Even if they are silent, they can still cause trouble, particularly if they are stirred up after holding back grievances for long periods. One method of making contact is the periodic use of a comment table in the dining room to ask for some spontaneous feedback. The dinner meal period is the best time for this approach, since people are less rushed and have the time for more casual conversation. For easy access, the table is set up near a high-traffic area with a couple of chairs handy to accommodate any passerby who wishes to have more time for a personal discussion. The table should display a well-designed sign prominently encouraging customers' comments about their food services. A poster or two relating to that fact near the entrances to the dining room is also a good idea to promote some participation. One or two of the food service managers and a resident representative normally attend the comment table. It is a team effort designed to attract anyone in the dining room who has a gripe or a suggestion and who does not have the time or desire to go through what they imagine to be a bureaucratic hassle. It is informally staged to draw in a good number of individuals over the course of the meal period. This approach is also a great icebreaker and a neat way to meet more customers. From then on, it is a lot easier to recognize previously met customers from earlier meal periods and to engage in some friendly discourse. All kinds of current events usually come up in conversation, so interactions with customers do not have to focus on shortcomings of the food services. Once people understand more about how their food service works and they get to know a manager as a real person, the food services takes on an improved persona. Besides, meeting and greeting can be fun, and it can be one of the added pleasures of working in food service.

After spending much time in the arena of institutional food service where the emphasis is on getting to know customers, it became apparent to me that this same philosophy was not prevalent in public restaurants, and I wondered why. It would seem the sensible thing to do, but when eating out it was seldom I observed anyone even resembling a manager visibly taking a personal interest in customer satisfaction. When someone did come to our table, the inquiry mostly came across rather mechanical, as if they were following some kind of script. It seemed they were most anxious to move on and away from our table quickly; as I imagined, it meant they wanted to avoid any unpleasant criticism. It is not that restaurant patrons care to be interrupted while halfway through savoring the main course, but there is a proper time to make an effective customer contact. An ideal time would be just after taking that first bite, when the food could be just right, not hot enough, too rare, or overcooked. The item could be corrected promptly, and the meal would continue. This may be difficult to accomplish for every table, but an alert waitperson can make a concerted effort. This is a great impression to make on the diner, who will come to judge an establishment's service as superb. If, due to time and circumstances, this early opportunity is missed, at least some inquiry should be made toward the end of the meal sometime between the final course or while waiting for the check. This is when a sincere inquiry with intent to listen may provide some valuable insight into how food services are truly performing. This requires some finesse and timing on the part of management, and you should understand there is a difference between being bothersome and being a good host. In the crowded restaurant industry, knowing the customers well can mean the difference in gaining that sought-after competitive edge.

If a restaurant owner or manager loves this crazy business, he or she should love the customers, too. In this sense, you should be highly motivated to get to know as many customers as possible. Do not count on large numbers of customers being close friends, but there is one thing that would put someone high on their list of acquaintances. The secret is to recognize them by name, and if you know the names of all your customers, it would be fantastic. It appears to be an awesome undertaking, but with a good game plan, it may not be so difficult after all. Find a scheme that fosters a certain amount of interaction that helps break the ice and makes it easier to get to know people as individuals.

One idea is to encourage customers to make reservations, if it is appropriate for the type of restaurant. In this way, you can begin to accumulate a solid list of customer names. Of course, if the business is so busy that taking reservations is a waste of time, just remember there will come a time when steady customers may have other reasons for not walking through the door anymore. Keep them coming back by contacting them about all the new and wonderful things in store for them. A personal file of customer names and numbers developed through a reservation policy can help do that. Cherish and preserve customers, especially during the good times when taking them for granted is tempting. One of the best things about asking for reservations is that you can greet a guest and his or her party by name upon their arrival. This group is going to be duly impressed, and they will remember. Also, to stimulate some additional goodwill, customers can be rewarded for making repeat reservations and showing up on time. At the management's discretion, they can be treated to a complimentary dessert or appetizer, depending on which fits the occasion. Better yet, provide them with a signed business card for a complimentary treat the next time they come to your establishment. For a $2 food cost investment, you will usually get a big smile, but an even more rewarding return is that next $30 or more check.

I think some restaurants are run by the introverts of the world who seem to go out of their way to avoid any face-to-face customer contact by furnishing that impersonal tabletop comment card. When were you last motivated to fill out one of those ridiculous, food-stained survey cards prominently displayed between the pepper shaker and the catsup bottle? If you have ever done so, do you ever remember receiving a response? For me, it never seemed to accomplish anything, and I always suspected the local management could easily manipulate any serious complaint before it went to their superiors.

True restaurateurs should be able to observe and evaluate for themselves their own level of food and service quality without relying on customer comment cards. However, there is some value in communicating in this manner, and there is a right way to do it. The first rule when using a customer comment card is that it must be conducted on a personal level, not simply left on a table or a counter just to avoid an embarrassing encounter. The technique succeeds best when a member of management or a wait person extends the comment card to the guest when he or she is leaving or paying the check with a remark about appreciating their input so the restaurant can strive to keep improving.

A simple 4-by-5-inch card will do, with four or five basic questions requiring a yes or no answer, plus one open-ended question and a brief comment line if desired. You may use this outline that follows, unless of course you want to get creative and make an original one.

CUSTOMER COMMENT CARD

Upon your entry into our establishment, (Restaurant's Name), were you and your guest or guests recognized promptly, and was your greeting friendly?

Yes____ No____ Comments_____

Did you find the menu selections appealing and reasonably priced?

Yes____ No____ Comments_____

Did you enjoy the taste, temperature, and the quality of your food?

Yes____ No____ Comments_____

Did you enjoy the service by our wait staff?

Yes____ No____ Comments_____

Is there anything you would suggest regarding any aspect of your dining experience that needs improvement or that you would wish to see done differently? _____

_____

_____

We appreciate your candor, and for your time and consideration, we intend to draw one comment card each month and award the winner a $20 credit on a dinner for two on their next visit.

Name_____ Telephone Number_____

Providing an added incentive of a drawing and the extent of the reward are strictly up to management. It sometimes makes sense to put a little lottery hype into the program to make it interesting, which is another opportunity to meet and learn the names of the winners. Running a busy restaurant is time consuming, but when doing something to actively interact with customers, it is time well spent. If you can force yourself out of your shell and make the effort, you will eventually discover the greater reward and have more fun doing it.

Compiling a list of customers' names undeniably takes time and effort, and to make the system work easier, it would be wise to enter the information into a computer for easy reference. From there you can embellish this directory with birthdays, anniversaries, children's names, favorite foods, and almost anything that will help recognize a customer as a favored patron. The task may appear overwhelming at first, but the idea is to start building data on a daily basis, and by being persistent, begin to see how fast the list begins to grow. Nothing is sweeter than the sound of a person's own name, and if you knew how few businesses even make the slightest effort, you would realize the potential competitive edge you can acquire if you make the commitment.

Do not think it is just an advantage for the owner or the general manager, for it may serve the individual employee an even greater personal benefit. Careers and job opportunities open up to those who demonstrate the best interpersonal skills, and recognizing people by using their proper names is at the top of the list. People who hold power remember those who give recognition to them, and powerful people have the means and the occasion to eat out a lot. You should not be surprised if you — this includes the wait staff, greeters, servers, cashiers, and especially assistant managers — are approached. The world is looking for talent, and there are few better places to shine. When relating well to the customers, you are in the spotlight, and you are being observed more than you might think. Business managers, owners, and human resource personnel are always on the hunt for good talent in this modern, competitive market. In life, it is a numbers game, and the more frequently you exhibit a warm personality, the more opportunities will start to present themselves. Call it luck, or being at the right place at the right time, but in reality it is just your turn to collect on your shining ability to give excellent personal service to others.

Building sales certainly has to be the number one objective for operating a successful business. An attractive menu, good food, value pricing, nice atmosphere, and good service are all major contributors to the sales effort and contribute to repeat business. Customers appreciate these positives and tend to favor those establishments by coming back on a frequent basis. It takes time to build up a good customer base, and when you have attained that level, why not put forth the extra effort to put an extra seal on your best customers' loyalty? Never take anything for granted in this business. One small slip in the quality or the service can swiftly send loyal customers to a competitor's establishment. It can happen whether operators want to admit it or not, and no matter how good they think they are, there will be bad days. Therefore, be aware that a possible decline in customer loyalty may someday come; it behooves you to have something in the "loyalty bank" to draw upon. Keep that bank balance positive by constantly providing your good customers with that extra personal touch. Get to know your customers, recognize them at first contact, and have techniques in place that demonstrate, in some fashion, appreciation for their business. It is intangible and hard to measure, but if ignored or left to chance it can cause customers to silently drift away.

Chapter 12

The Kitchen

(It is not General Motors, but it is a factory.)

Those who are just beginning a career in food service management or who have been limited to experiences in smaller operations can have some real apprehensions about operating a large, institutional kitchen. Having this level of responsibility thrust upon you all at once without some background can be intimidating. For this reason, new managers who naturally have early feelings of inadequacy tend to stay away from the back of the house food production process. One obstacle is the fear of having to deal with the old-hand cooks, who may have been on the job since the new, young manager was in diapers. I felt that same exact way — in awe of this large kitchen and anxious — on my first assignment as the food production manager.

I kept asking myself how in the world I was going to direct these workers if I did not know the first thing about how to operate any of these monster machines. I knew something about forecasting production, ordering food supplies, recipe preparation procedures, and record-keeping, but this array of enormous and strange equipment baffled me. I began working in the kitchen doing the things I was trained to do and concentrated my time where I could be productive on the things I knew how to do best. After a while my nerves started to settle down, and by not pretending to know it all, a good working relationship began to develop between the kitchen staff and me. Surprisingly, no one asked me about operating the kitchen equipment, the one thing I feared most.

It then suddenly dawned on me that it was not my job to know everything about everything. I was not expected to operate the equipment. I was expected to function as the manager, fulfilling the duties I was specifically trained for. The job of the manager is to support the food production process and to support the workers, not do their jobs. It is the reason for having an organization made up of people with a variety of different skills and knowledge who, by working together as a team, successfully produce a product or a service. What makes the system work is the coordination of all these activities toward one specific goal. The mission of any food service organization is to prepare and serve the best possible food for its customers with style and efficiency, and as any boss will remind the employees: "Better to do it within the forecasted food and labor budget."

Learning this concept about the division of duties and skills in operating a kitchen was a revelation that has helped me throughout my entire management career. It was not necessary for me to be an expert about everything except on how to be an effective manager of people. I was no longer fearful of taking on larger assignments and opening new food service facilities. It was the realization that every individual comes with certain abilities, and by teaming them with others of equal ability, an organized system of quality food production and service can be established. I have learned it is best to use a person's strength, rather than trying to correct or change an inherent weakness. In simple terms, some people are just good at baking cakes while others excel in customer service. The job of management is to extract and direct these strengths from the people best able to deliver them. When we try to make people into something they are not, we are wasting everybody's time, and both our customer and our business turn out to be the loser.

Getting back to the subject of kitchen equipment, it was not long before I gradually acquired a fairly good working knowledge of the basic operation. It took some careful observation and some hands-on experience. Those massive-looking kettles turned out not to be as complicated as I first thought. I began asking questions and found out, if employees are approached properly, they will not become defensive. They were helpful, and everyone seemed to appreciate the attention. Though it was not necessary for me to be an expert in every detail of food preparation, it was important for me to know some of the key fundamentals, especially for sanitation and safety purposes. However, the kitchen employees were most competent, and I came to respect their skills, as they in turn depended on me. My advice to the new and upcoming food service managers is not to avoid the kitchen production area because of any feelings of inadequacy. Everyone is inadequate in something, and that also goes for those who have been in the business for a long time. It is when you do not know that you do not know that can get you into real trouble.

Some people are brought up with the idea that they should not be telling their employees to do something on the job that they have not done themselves or even mastered. That might be appropriate in certain limited situations, but if we had to wait for all that to happen, the world would not make much progress. Few want to wait another 20 years to acquire skills that, as a manager, they will not have the time to use anyway. The industry needs good food service managers now, not later, so do not be afraid to take on new responsibilities. You can work and be involved successfully in any kitchen production area, as long as you know clearly what quality standards are expected and you have some basic knowledge about production and sanitation. Good managers can communicate those expectations and, by using their best leadership skills, can direct their fulfillment.

Kitchens come in all shapes and sizes, and unfortunately, some I have seen have turned out to be real killers. Having to walk your legs off or continually having to climb stairs working in one of these monstrosities can wear down the best of us. If you are unlucky at some time in your career, you may have the opportunity to try to make a difficult kitchen work. You may wonder how anyone in their right mind could have designed this nightmare in which you are supposed to produce meals with some semblance of efficiency. Exposure to poorly planned kitchens should be minimal, and most people in the industry can only hope that the majority of these kitchens have disappeared from the scene. The only possible benefit is learning some hard lessons while trying to operate one of these lemons.

Poor kitchen design is usually the result of not first taking into consideration what purpose the facility is supposed to accomplish in the first place. Administrators of larger institutions, particularly in the educational and healthcare fields, sometimes do not give adequate attention to the detailed food service requirements of their new building projects. Building architects are usually not qualified in the specialty of kitchen facilities design, and therefore, the services of a certified food facilities designer should be enlisted for this purpose. An extra expense perhaps, but over time, the investment will save countless dollars by having a plan that maximizes customer participation, provides an efficient flow of food production, and minimizes labor expenses.

In addition, the administrator should ask for input from his or her own food service director and key staff members, along with an outside consultant to ensure that the planned kitchen layout will achieve the food service department's long-term objectives. A certain amount of flexibility must also be built into the design, so future equipment and service concept changes can be made without structural restrictions and excessive costs. Institutional facilities, by nature, are built like the Rock of Gibraltar and soon become dated. Food services must be able to change with the trends and future customer demands, if the operation is to remain viable as well as efficient.

Before even starting to think about designing a kitchen facility, think about the customers who are going to be served, the type of menu, and the service that will be most needed. This makes sense, but in many cases, the thought process seems to run backward. The approach is sometimes to build a kitchen that fits the allotted space and then let the operators make it work. That is faulty thinking and primed for failure. An intelligent, well-coordinated design is the key, because once construction specifications are set, it is over. An important element of the plan is to determine a realistic estimate of the number of patrons the facility is expected to service. The kitchen should be large enough and adequately equipped to efficiently produce and deliver the required menu, but not too large so the staff members have to run their legs off. High labor productivity is critical to the profitability of any food service operation, and an inappropriate kitchen design can doom the venture before the first meal is even served.

Before drawing up a kitchen layout, begin by reviewing the menu concept, taking into consideration the two most important factors. The first is to determine all the necessary steps required to produce every menu item, and the second is to project the maximum volume of meals expected to be served. Then, proceed to compile a basic list of the equipment needed, and determine how the pieces will fit together. Regardless of knowledge and experience, do not try to do this project alone. This is an extremely complex process to get right. Engage as many qualified people as possible who are related to the project to help think through the many details and to decide on the best options.

The following is a guide on the makeup of a basic kitchen facility:

Starting with the cook's station there should be a stove, oven, grill, fryer, a handy shelf to hold spices and herbs, a unit to keep cooked food hot, accessible refrigeration, an adequate sink, and a workable service counter from which the wait staff can easily pick up orders. Everything should be within arm's reach to be efficient and minimize steps. Larger operations that require more than one cook's station may separate the functions of grilling, frying, or sautéing, depending on the menu requirements.

The pantry station should be equipped for salad preparation and easy pickup service. This will require adequate refrigeration, sink, and counter workspace. If baking is not done on location, this area would also handle the portioning and serving of the menu dessert items.

The beverage station should be large enough and easily accessible for the wait staff to fill all the beverages the menu offers. Adequate space needs to be provided for fresh ice and the ready supply of clean beverage service ware or disposables. It is important to avoid creating a bottleneck at what will be a busy workstation. Give designing this location a lot of thought.

The soiled dish return station should be conveniently located for the wait staff returning from the dining areas but not be congested, which could cause accidents and breakage. A machine dishwasher or a three-compartment sink for hand dishwashing should adjoin the space allocated for segregating and scraping the soiled service ware. A pre-rinsing sink is a critical addition, and a garbage disposal is useful at this location if management decides it is advantageous to have one.

Safety regulations require that all cleaning chemicals be stored separately from all food supplies. Therefore, a self-contained area with a heavy-duty utility sink is imperative for all kitchens that require daily cleaning. This is the place to clean and store mops and buckets and to dispose of dirty mop water. The space should be adequate to store brooms, dustpans, trash bags, and shelving to neatly keep all necessary cleaning supplies in order.

Food storage areas require at least 25 percent of the total space allocated for the kitchen layout. This will include space for dry storage, refrigeration, and freezer items. When adequate storage space is left out of the kitchen design, it hampers the operation and causes extra work for the kitchen staff. You will feel quite irritated by this when trying to find something packed into an 80-cubic foot freezer designed to support a 500-seat cafeteria. It becomes difficult to rotate the stock to ensure freshness, and attempts to take advantage of lower prices through volume purchasing are virtually impossible.

These are costly design errors, which can be avoided if experienced food service operators are invited to participate in the original planning process. Further, some of the old-time kitchen employees can provide some valuable insight if the people in charge of the project take the time to ask a few questions. It is just one more input for consideration when trying to create a workable kitchen design.

A disciplined approach for receiving food and supply deliveries is critical for controlling food costs. There should be ample space near the rear entrance to the kitchen for a designated receiving area. Anywhere from 30 to 45 percent of total food sales equates to the cost of the food purchased. Ultimately, this total dollar value must be received and accounted for through the back door. It is not a job that should be treated lightly because suppliers sometimes make errors in shipments, and they need to be challenged. The quality of highly perishable products must be inspected, and this responsibility for control still lies with the individual.

Proper receiving may rank in the top three most important aspects of food cost control and is most certainly not a function to be delegated to an untrained employee. Many dollars pass through the back door, and it is not just in terms of the number of boxes, but in verifying accurate weights, ensuring the correct product specification as ordered, and guaranteeing the freshness and quality of raw products. A responsible person, most preferably an experienced manager or chef, should take control of the receiving process. In support of the process, the purchase and use of a good receiving scale is a worthwhile investment that will pay for itself in short order. Also, suppliers and delivery people are quick to learn respect for businesses that pay close attention to receiving practices. It is more likely that additional care will be taken of those customers who are most particular about correct shipments and who pay close personal attention to accepting deliveries only as specified. If there is a show of slackness, eventually careless business practices can become an invitation to being dumped on.

A working desk, telephone, and a place for a file cabinet in the kitchen area, which is partially enclosed with good visibility of the work area, is desirable and essential to good organization. Though often an overlooked detail, it is by no means a luxury, but an important necessity. The kitchen is a production center requiring attention to the menu, recipes, training guides, work schedules, personnel records, purchasing specs, invoices, and other important information. Without ample office space allocation in the kitchen, the operation can easily slip into chaos. The long hours and a life working in a kitchen are difficult enough. It is wise to arrange for some semblance of order and efficiency.

Whether purchasing a food service business from a seller, building a new one, or even going through some major facility renovation, you will need to deal with local government regulators. Before submitting any final designs to a contractor, it would be wise to run the plans by the local health department or the agency that will be responsible for issuing a permit to operate. All inspectors place particular emphasis on certain requirements, though all follow standard health protection regulations. They will be able to give advice up front before beginning to make a big investment, such as whether the plan complies with local, state, and federal food facility codes. Often a plan may require only a moderate change that may avoid a heavy expense if done later. Accept these rules in a positive way and cooperate fully with all the officials that are encountered. It will serve you well and will smooth out the entire process in obtaining a business license with minimum delays.

Chapter 13

Owning Your Own Business

(How to prepare for it and build it right.)

Almost everyone who aspires to enter the food service industry thinks seriously at one time or another about the possibility of owning and operating a restaurant. Doing so is the ultimate of dreams, and traditionally it has been bred into many as the American ideal. However, it may be a good idea to first reflect on what is involved and how to best prepare yourself. Many people have the misconception that, just because they are a whiz at cooking or mom's recipes are worth a million, they are just a step away from creating a gold mine of a restaurant. Those who proceed solely on this basis are ill prepared to face the real world of business and often find themselves headed for disaster. Dreams are wonderful, but you must keep at least one foot firmly on the ground.

To some degree, almost everyone is a self-proclaimed expert on the right way and the wrong way to run a restaurant based on their patronization of restaurants. People imagine that all it takes is some common sense and a strong desire to do it. It looks easy. Unfortunately, the failure rate of new restaurants is astoundingly high. Even many of the well-established ones lose their luster over time and eventually close. Their struggle with survival suggests that a few things are possibly being overlooked.

Besides the money and some terrific ability, maybe the most essential requirement for opening a restaurant business is courage. Undoubtedly, it takes quite a person to undertake the enormous risk and responsibility of starting such an enterprise. Above all, it requires a person with many talents, or at least one who knows how to assemble and pull together the various skills and capabilities required to operate a successful restaurant.

In essence, you will be in the business of manufacturing a variety of products that are highly perishable for customers of various taste preferences, who are unpredictable about which items they will select and without any guarantees that they will even show up. There will be times when the refrigerator breaks down, the delivery does not arrive on time, the cook walks out, the waitress slips and falls, the accountant suddenly leaves the country, and the drain pipes back up. The list goes on. The statistics are stacked against the budding entrepreneur. Most people, upon hearing this "encouragement," will come to their senses and decide it is best not to give up their day jobs. However, for those few courageous people who are well-prepared and relentlessly driven, there could be no better feeling of accomplishment and pride than from opening and sustaining their own business.

Money and knowledge are the two basic requirements you should seriously consider before starting out alone. How much money depends on the size and scope of the operation you intend to operate. Once you have determined that figure, you ought to double it. This will be a more realistic amount required, for nothing seems to emerge more unexpectedly than the opening expenses of a startup venture. An opening is not just for the first day, either. It is for weeks, maybe months before customer sales can be built to a level that can produce a reasonable profit and all operating inefficiencies have been corrected. Knowledge is just as important. We can all say we have experience, but that does not mean it is the right kind. Be prepared with those two basic requirements of adequate financing and knowledge, and you will have a decent chance to succeed.

To be primed with the right kind of knowledge, first determine the type of restaurant or food service operation that most appeals to you. Then, search out similar restaurants to obtain some practical hands-on experience. If you aspire to own a table service restaurant, do not waste your time working in fast food places. Keep focusing on your goal of acquiring the specific knowledge and experience that you will need to succeed. Do not get sidetracked to other avenues where your time and effort will be wasted. Sometimes, it is difficult to stay the course when other factors, such as family, friends, and finances, draw heavily on your time and spirit. Be prepared to face some challenges to overcome the hard times, even though you may feel alone. This is the price and personal sacrifice required of those who wish to reach their goal of independence.

Once you have set your sights on where to obtain some practical experience, it is preferable to work at least on two levels in the type of restaurant you would like to own. Having a cook's position is helpful, but your understanding of the business is enhanced if you can gain some work experience as the assistant manager or above. Likewise, many a good waitperson has gone on to own and operate a successful business. However, these folks have wisely supplemented that experience with some additional business training. Try gaining some experience at a variety of relative jobs that will expand your perspective and knowledge. Those who have had the opportunity to work in several establishments at various levels before venturing out are well ahead in terms of being prepared.

If you also have some academic training from a community college, a technical school, or a higher level, so much the better. A little book theory along with work experience is a good combination to have, and it will multiply your knowledge and ability to help you make good decisions in the future. In addition, there is a lot to learn from the mistakes other people make. That is, if you are a good student who learns well from observation and who constantly thinks about ways to improve the way things work. Always learning and trying new ideas is essential in an industry in which the perception and fickleness of the public often determine who succeeds and who does not.

The second requirement, no less important than ability, is the matter of money. It takes adequate investment capital to start up a new enterprise or to purchase an up-and-running business from another owner. Never forget about the additional funds to cover the critical operating costs that are required at the early stages of a new startup. A business does not start making a profit right off the bat, and cutting it too close has been the downfall of many a budding entrepreneur. A grand opening may seem unbelievably successful. The joint is jumping, and the customers are wall to wall. This appears to be the beginning of a success, but the cost of advertising, opening promotions, hiring and training all new employees, and the inefficiencies and mistakes of just getting started will be taking a heavy toll.

Many kinks still have to be worked out even after implementing the best of opening plans. Operating costs still have to be linked and aligned with daily sales fluctuations if a business is expected to grow and earn adequate profits. Management's strict attention to the details of where the money is going is imperative, for at this early stage it is easy to get off track in a short period of time.

At some point you may begin to realize that having too much experience and knowledge about all the requirements and inherent problems about owning your own business can be an impediment. You may begin to focus more on the risks involved and all the things that can go wrong than on the potential rewards. This is where the element of desire comes into play. Are you capable of overcoming these apprehensions and willing to go forward in this venture?

You may discover that being an independent entrepreneur does not work well for you. It is not for everyone, and there are viable alternatives. People who, by nature, need a degree of independence and are endowed with a strong entrepreneurial spirit can have grand and prosperous careers in both large and small corporations. The smart companies that adhere to this philosophy see to it that their style of management and personnel policies are in place to attract those types of individuals. In the right environment, it is quite possible for an individual manager to enjoy the spirit of independence while still working for a large organization. When managers who run their frontline units are given a measure of freedom and the flexibility to make decisions on their own, they develop a degree of self-reliance and a greater sense of responsibility for attaining results. It can be the best of both worlds, being an entrepreneur and having the benefits of a broad support system while working for a large organization. It is in this sense that the frontline manager can gain that terrific feeling of being in business for him- or herself. The best of companies do promote this philosophy of management, so look for one if this is a desirable step toward reaching your goal.

No one ever made it big in the restaurant business without a lot of help. Unless starting out small, such as a one-person hole in the wall, you will always be in the personnel business. Even the so-called mom-and-pops must deal with the issue of developing a satisfactory working relationship between themselves and their employees. A business requires attention to innumerable details, and the heavy service demands constantly put individuals under various levels of stress. This can be particularly intense when it relates to financial issues. Also, disagreements can turn volatile without some kind of mutual understanding concerning business practices and policies. Therefore, before opening a new business, everyone involved needs to agree on and accept the ground rules. It may take a lot of compromising to grind out an agreeable, workable plan, but it is better to be done ahead of time rather than later. Disruptions later can be damaging and sometimes fatal to a fledgling business. Avoid this disruptive situation by putting time into writing a business plan and, just as important, a detailed outline of policies and procedures. They must be addressed in advance if future conflicts are to be avoided. It is a mistake to believe that misunderstandings can easily be worked out after the business is underway.

THE TYPICAL BUSINESS PLAN SHOULD INCLUDE:

1. Sales projections for at least the first year, month by month.

2. Cost projections in detail for labor, food, and direct expenses for the same period.

   - A labor cost analysis, including a working schedule for all employees.

   - A menu pre-cost analysis and pricing schedule.

   - A list of suppliers with estimated price quotes for major menu items.

   - Quotes for all required insurances, utility estimates, rents, leases, and licenses.

3. A demographic study of the proposed business location.

4. A marketing plan to reach potential customers.

5. A plan and a budget for advertising.

6. A capital investment budget and sources for capital.

7. A capital operating budget.

8. A grand opening plan and budget.

9. A list of key employees with résumés.

POLICIES AND PROCEDURES SHOULD INCLUDE:

1. A job description of duties and responsibilities for all positions, including management.

2. Personnel policies:

   - A schedule of pay rates by position, based on annual market comparisons.

   - A schedule for performance reviews and pay rate actions.

   - An outline of bonus opportunities and special award programs.

   - Sanitation and housekeeping procedures, with assigned cleaning responsibilities.

   - A list of rules and an outline of steps for discipline and correction.

   - Discharge procedures consistent with required reviews and the labor laws.

3. Purchasing and receiving procedures, specifications, par levels, storage, and security.

4. Procedures for conducting monthly inventories.

5. Cash handling, cashier controls, record-keeping, and banking.

6. Monthly review of operating statements, budget comparisons, and corrective action plans.

7. A periodic review schedule by management of all policies and procedures.

Any business enterprise, no matter how small, should at least be able to decide on some basic policies and procedures and have them put into writing. These should be well-thought-out statements that provide a guide for consistency and a means to address daily problems, while minimizing conflict and misunderstandings. However, they do not have to be inflexible. Policies should be reviewed and updated periodically, so they are applicable to changing conditions. In addition, management requires some degree of flexibility when having to deal with exceptional circumstances.

As independent business operations become larger, it may be necessary to expand and separate policies and procedures into distinct manuals. You should avoid the proliferation of large and wordy policy and procedure manuals generated by a corporation's home office executives, which are more for their own purposes than for what these manuals are intended to accomplish.

The primary purposes are to assist frontline operations in staying on track, outlining well-thought-out actions that promote efficiency, and obtaining the desired results. The frontline operators should have a say in keeping operating policies and procedures valid and up to date. Large corporations sometimes forget that people in the field have some insight and experience worth hearing. If home office executives are the types who get carried away with their own importance, they may cringe about the idea of allowing field operating managers too much participation in developing operating procedures. Their fears of losing control are unwarranted, and their actions can be suppressive to creativity. They need to be reminded at times that the most important part of leadership is creating an environment in which frontline management people can fully exercise their hard-earned skills and intelligence. The best executives are those who allow the creativity of their best people, instead of hindering it. Smart leaders come to realize, by fostering participatory management, it is also nurturing their own development toward further management growth. Moreover, they are guilty of wasting a valuable resource by attempting to dictate only what they think is best for frontline personnel. It does not mean that executives should not actively contribute the benefits of their own experience and judgment during the process, but the primary authors must be those who will ultimately have the task of making operating procedures work every day in the real world. If the management in the field has the opportunity to participate, the chance for the implementation of practical and worthy operating procedures is enhanced. If necessary, the home office support staff can correct the spelling, tidy the language, and bind it up into a readable package. Do not have these important tools collect dust on the back bookshelves because they have become irrelevant or too bulky to assimilate.

Since management turnover is an unpleasant fact, policies and procedures should be reviewed at least every two years. The people involved will likely be different, and they too must be ready to assume some authorship and personal responsibility. If the enterprise is to remain vibrant and continue to grow successfully, it is imperative that the new operating team makes the necessary adjustments to suit new technology, the changing market, and the current business conditions.

Even the small, independent business enterprises need to think in larger terms when it comes to organization, the division of responsibilities, operating procedures, and long-term goals. If you are going to be successful in owning your own business, you should take some lessons from the professionals who have made it big. Have a sensible plan in writing, be financially prepared to weather the opening storms, and choose employees wisely. Allow them to share in the development of high operating standards, and keep everyone focused on providing the best possible service to customers. If you have the courage to begin, the wisdom to be well prepared, and the perseverance to stay the course, you will be well rewarded.

Chapter 14

Leadership Your Employees Can Respect

(Determining the right approach for dealing with your fellow humans.)

The most frequent comment about the nature of the food service industry is, "We're not in the food business, we're in the people business." It is undeniable that food service people and their performance is one of the most critical factors that determine whether a business succeeds or fails. It is not just in food service, for without people and their skills, loyalty, and enthusiastic attitudes, any business enterprise will have trouble surviving.

Effective management is about good leadership, and leaders take people in the direction in which success and benefits are available to everyone. The first step is to define the mission in clear terms. Just as important, good leaders must take the time to tell their employees about the mission of the business and how everyone's job fits into accomplishing it. If they do not get the right message at the beginning of their employment then management has simply failed to communicate. The violators of this basic tenet for management abound, and examples are rampant in the food service industry. It may be a hard thing to admit, but no other business more neglects the building of good employee attitudes, while at the same time complaining about the quality of their help, than food service employers.

The help wanted signs in windows are nothing more than a crap shoot and attest to the simplistic disregard some employers give to the importance of recruiting the right people and then building on the right attitudes. This is a hurried type of business, but that should not be an excuse. To the misfortune of many food service businesses, the lack of good leadership and the inability to foster enthusiasm for excellent customer service has caused more failures than many managers are willing to admit. It is obvious that food service workers must have good attitudes if the business is to flourish. If this basic standard is a necessity for the business to prosper, it would seem common sense for food service managers to excel in the area of personnel development. Managers who understand this need and communicate with patience and respect for those they instruct enjoy not only business success, but also the good feeling that comes from developing people to their full potential. This is an excellent opportunity for those who aspire to influence and lead people to a higher level of productivity and ultimately to a better standard of living.

To some, the mystery of food preparation, whether it be a science or an art, can be rather intimidating. This mystification has been traditionally fostered by the chefs of old who were not about to share their command and total control of "their kitchen." Though examples of kitchen despots are rare today, the complexity of the back of the house still remains somewhat of a hurdle for the new food service manager. The chef is certainly a key player, but the responsibility for the bottom line usually falls on the shoulders of the manager. Since the major cost factor for most food service operations is the cost of food prepared in the kitchen, it behooves the manager to be well-versed in the details of food cost control. If you think it requires years of kitchen experience and special hands-on training to be a good business manager, you have been misinformed. It may not be the best place to receive a good education on keeping food costs on budget because the chef and his staff are sometimes motivated differently than the business owners. The chef and preparation people tend to be more like artists who receive their greatest satisfaction from creating a variety of tasty and visually appealing dishes. Unfortunately, the chef's favorites may not be as exciting to customers in certain markets. The management, while in support of this ideal of chef artistry, must also deal with the reality of operating a business and making a profit. Keeping things in balance requires constant attention given to the cost of ingredients, portion control, minimizing waste, and keeping menu prices at a reasonable level to attract sufficient customers. Though managers and chefs are sometimes at odds, their respective special talents and skills are important ingredients to the ultimate success of the operation. This is where cooperation and a mutual respect for each other are of critical importance. Think of it as a marriage of sorts that will blend the diverse skills and knowledge of both partners. This is a necessity for keeping the business on a successful course.

It is a wonderful asset to have highly skilled and dedicated people in the kitchen producing great food. They are an inspiration and are most valuable for this purpose, and a smart manager will be grateful for having such talent. By showing sincere appreciation for this special ability, a manager will be earning the respect of the kitchen staff, thereby opening the door for good communication. It is important to realize that no single person is blessed with all the skills and answers. Be a realist, and do not expect the impossible. It makes more sense to build on an individual's strength rather than on his or her weakness. To be openly critical of an employee's shortcomings is a turnoff, and it certainly does not foster a willingness to listen or to cooperate. You can only obtain an employee's undivided attention when he or she is are willing to give it, but to do this, management must be willing to give some first. It may take a little more time and patience to create the right rapport, but in the end it is worth the effort. The process of building teamwork can function only when the members come to understand that each individual has an important role to play. When there is an atmosphere of understanding and respect for each other's unique talents, the common goals of food quality and cost control can be achieved.

Almost everyone in the industry firmly supports the premise that some practical experience in the kitchen is a good primer for those interested in pursuing a career in food service management. With luck, this experience will be with a true professional so you will not pick up a lot of bad habits early on. Be aware of what is being taught and what makes sense. Realize that most people do not have the option to choose for whom they work, for what they may need at the time is a job, any job. Simply remember there is a lot more to learn about the business of food management than knowing how to prepare a terrific veal scaloppini. One of the best things about kitchen experience is gaining appreciation for the skills of the food production workers and the demanding aspects of the work. Too often they are unappreciated as well as underpaid, which I consider an omen for eventual business failure.

Sound management contains the elements of applied science and good organization, but it is also the practice of dealing effectively with employees. Those people who work hard in the kitchen regardless of their station deserve individual attention and respect. I find it a disturbing experience to witness a manager who exhibits a total disregard for his or her workforce. I have heard many management people who should know better make some disparaging remarks about their employees. In essence, they are casting blame on others for their own managerial mistakes. It is no wonder they never seem to succeed.

A important thing managers must learn is to take the time to listen to their food preparation and service employees, and that means every one of them. Managers have a tendency to talk too much; this is because of the pressure they are under to get a lot done in a short time, and to accomplish this they need to communicate many instructions. This is undeniably a necessity, but if it is all one-way communication, you could be missing some valuable input from the employees. Management does not always have all the right answers, and to hold fast to this assumption is rather foolhardy. It feels good when someone asks for advice. It makes sense, then, to tap into the knowledge of the people who are in the midst of handling the details of their job. Do not be shy; just ask, and it is probable that employees can uncover some things to get the job done a lot better than their boss ever thought of. By sharing ideas and communicating on the same level, something good happens: two people on the same wavelength working together to accomplish an objective of mutual benefit. I guarantee a smile will emerge, and you will discover a person much more willing to contribute. You have made someone else feel important. If one works for someone, he or she must be necessary, and therefore, by definition, must be important; otherwise you would be overstaffing. A good pot washer is just as important to the success of any restaurant as the salad maker is. Everyone has a job to do; a breakdown anywhere in the system jeopardizes the entire operation, and everyone eventually pays the price.

The practical incentive for respecting employees and building their self-esteem is that it translates into superior performance. Their sense of self-worth is no different from the manager's. When given their due, they tend to become a supporter and thereby are motivated to help the business succeed. Employees will either make you or break you, and most prefer the former. Think logically of all the many things that can possibly occur during the production process, which is literally impossible to supervise as a whole. For example, not taking the time to measure recipe ingredients, cooking at too high a temperature, over-portioning, not adhering to production requirements, not properly rotating food products in refrigerators and freezers, wasting time, and the taking of a thousand shortcuts. Any of these infractions can be severely detrimental to food quality and can drive up costs, which will not be recovered easily. You need employees to look after your best interests, but that will not happen unless you start by taking a sincere interest in their best interests.

The best advice I ever received when I was assigned to my first major responsibility was to start out by getting to know all my employees on an individual basis. Being new at managing, I had previously heard an opposite point of view. There were admonitions that it was imperative for management to establish a strong authority on day one and let the employees know who was boss. Perhaps even fire one or two just to set an example and to prove that you are a tough-minded manager who does not tolerate any nonsense. Some leaders still believe that is the way to lead, but fortunately those ideas are becoming extinct. It was a traditional style in years past, and do not be too surprised if you come across a few of those advocates even today. Weak managers seem to have a need to prove their authority, and unfortunately, what they do not understand is the practice they subscribe to is counterproductive. It takes them a long time, if ever, to change their ways. Even with my inexperience, I did not think that was the best approach for dealing with fellow humans. Perhaps it was due to an old-fashioned upbringing and all the good examples set by my parents, grandparents, uncles, and aunts. Then, when I received good coaching from management on how to succeed with my new employees by emphasizing the building of good relationships, I felt confident about moving forward. It is scary enough to start out on one's first big assignment without having a hostile workforce to boot. I needed their support.

Going through an introduction ritual is the first order of business when management changes take place. In the process, an employee meeting is called, whereupon someone of higher rank introduces the new manager. A few remarks are made to remind everyone of the importance of each person's efforts in accordance with company policy and the need to cooperate with the new manager. Then, the new manager, usually with shaky knees, will express his or her pleasure with having this new opportunity to serve and with sincere intent says something about looking forward to working closely with everyone present. Nice words, but employees overall are natural skeptics because they have heard the same bland speeches many times before and, from experience, know that few positive changes ever come about after the usual pontifications from the higher-ups.

The typical employee meeting for the most part makes the manager feel important, and it does require a certain amount of courage to stand up and speak in front of a new group of strangers. The mission is proclaimed with an appeal for everyone's cooperation, and the word teamwork, as usual, is always emphasized during these rituals. These first formal encounters are intended to impress, but the one most impressed is usually the speaker. Perhaps a few do somehow become captivated by your inspired words, but far more you may observe by their body language are not quite ready to buy into your program. I am not trying to belittle the introductory process and the importance of speaking out in front of new employees, because it is a good thing to do; however, this is just the beginning in establishing your role as a leader. Just because you have made a few charismatic statements in an employee meeting does not mean all your disciples are ready and motivated to fulfill every command. From now on, it takes the real work of getting to know people, learning from each other, and getting the job done right.

For many starting out on their first management assignment, it can be a time of grim apprehension. Most of this anxiety merely comes from not knowing how the newly assigned employees are going to react. Questions arise from the overactive imagination. Most wonder if employees will respond to directions or ignore them. These anxieties are normal, and most people will not sleep well the night before the first day on a new job. My advice is to try not to become overwhelmed with your own self-importance. The first day is the pinnacle for neither the new manager nor the ultimate future of the business. This is not the final match at the Olympics, and it is certainly not going to be the end of the world. It is just another day that will begin and end at the usual time, and you will have that feeling of relief when it is over. Try not to be too apprehensive, and accept the fact that a little fear is beneficial and that the impending rush of adrenaline makes you more alert and energetic. However, it is also important to be composed and attentive. Realize it is a day of orientation to learn the business and to meet new people, so relax and try to enjoy it. A lot of it depends on being on your best behavior and willing to listen more than you talk. It is a time to be asking questions and learning new things. After you know a little more about the operation and where you can best contribute, it will be time to start giving instructions.

Do not worry about establishing a strong leadership role the first day, barking out orders, and trying to impress everybody with your position of authority. The first job is to find out what makes things work. Try to learn who contributes and who is there just for the paycheck. Most of the time, employees will be trying to figure the new boss out. Perhaps they are not impressed at all and will choose to ignore you instead. The first days of a new management assignment are the best opportunity to sell yourself and to get your message across. Openly share expectations in clear language and mean it. Short but informative meetings with small groups or individuals on a daily basis are a good way to foster the communication process. It relaxes the tension for both parties, and perhaps some of the real concerns will naturally surface.

Invariably, at least one of the more assertive employees will ask for a raise or claim one was promised by a predecessor. Be prepared to field this one using the utmost composure. It will be a test of your ability to listen, sympathize, and investigate. Be willing to look into their concern, and be sure to get back to them with the appropriate answer. The correct response usually entails a calm review of the policy and an explanation of the correct time for wage reviews and performance appraisals. By promptly communicating an intelligent answer and standing firm, you will be regarded as someone who cannot be easily manipulated.

Do not patronize, but be respectful when responding to the inquiry. The objective is not to put down the employee, but to create an understanding about the fairness of the policy for all concerned. Smile and be upbeat. It is contagious, it creates enthusiasm, and it is certainly the kind of attitude made for the service business. Just treat the employees how you expect them to treat each other and yourself. This attitude will clearly show concern and interest in the welfare of others. When you get that across in the right manner, you will be well on your way to earning their respect as a leader.

In the real world, there will be employees who lie, cheat, and steal — and not necessarily those who are stationed at the lower levels. At the higher-held positions there is more lying, cheating, and stealing. However, it is a mistake to think that all employees in the food service industry are untrustworthy, and as a result, it is even worse for management to develop a negative attitude about employees as individuals. Do not let a few bad apples spoil your outlook about everyone else. Some employees are simply not going to be right, and the best thing for both parties is to have an amicable separation. Sometimes, it is due to differences in personality, an attitude problem, or someone having a separate agenda. If there is friction, everyone senses it, and this negative atmosphere does not lend itself to high productivity and good service.

Do not make it a big deal. If the employment arrangement is not working out for both parties, change it. This is why it is important to have a trial period for all new employees to become adjusted to a new working situation and to get in step to the new way of running things. It is for the benefit of the employee just as much as for the employer, and the employee who does not fit in has far more to lose. The employee categorized as marginal is not recognized, appreciated, or given opportunities for additional training and advancement. Further, employees not held in high regard are not given much attention. It is a common tendency for managers to ignore employees they do not like or find uncooperative, and it is a mannerism most employers cannot disguise. Being disregarded breeds resentment and fosters poor working habits, which ultimately leads to an employee quitting or being fired. People naturally work better for bosses who make them feel as if they are important and who regard them as winners.

If you cannot develop all the employees into winners, it becomes that much more difficult to be a top competitor in the field. The employee regards the manager as the person who holds the key to the future and is someone the employee wants to look up to and respect. People need good leaders and examples to follow. Therefore, every manager's personal key to success has to be how well he or she can fill this important role.

Chapter 15

The Essence of Management

(Miracle results by matching the right person to the job.)

I entered one of the major fast food chain restaurants for a quick meal on the road, expecting the usual food and service, but something was different. There was a refreshing sense of sharpness in the atmosphere that was above the norm. It was not a grand opening. None of the big brass were present with all their attentiveness and happy-to-see-you smiles. This place was in business for some time, but did not reflect the typical shop-worn appearance one might expect. The entrance was spotless, the queuing railings were shiny, and the floor, both carpet and tile, was immaculate. A good first impression, but it was even nicer to be greeted by a well-groomed service attendant asking for my order and, for a pleasant change, not chewing gum at the same time. The food was prepared and served quickly, and I noticed someone who appeared to be a member of management — the tie was a dead giveaway — involved in directing a efficient group of food service workers.

Next, the condiment station was well stocked, neatly arranged, and clean.

Heading for my table, I happened to notice the salad bar presentation, which had been discontinued at most of the units of this particular restaurant chain. I assumed it was because of the extra amount of work and attention it takes to maintain a fresh-looking salad bar throughout the day, or maybe someone at the company headquarters decided it was not adequately contributing to the bottom line. It was too bad; it was a nice feature to counterbalance the burgers and fries.

Perhaps, if the right amount of effort was put toward maintaining quality in the first place, the customers would have responded with their continued patronage, and the salad bar service would have been a winner for the company, not a financial drain. Somewhere along the line, it started out as a good idea designed to increase store activity but ultimately failed for no other reason than lack of attention. This obviously did not seem to be a problem at this particular operation. The salad bar was filled with a attractive variety of fresh items, which an attendant replenished on a regular basis. Each container was clean and filled to the right level. It was so well done and appealing that I was sorry I had decided not to choose the salad bar for my lunch that day.

When seated at my table, I was pleased when opening my wrapped sandwich, noticing it was hot, fresh, and neatly assembled. Most of the time, you think the assembly prep people were trying to break some kind of fast food speed record. As I observed the dining area, I did not notice a single table that needed cleaning, though the restaurant was fairly busy at midday. On top of that, there was a neatly written message on every table informing customers that they were invited here to eat, not to clean tables. Apparently, they did not believe customers should bus tables. From all appearances, it looked as if they took care of this added service and, again, the operation did not appear to be overstaffed in the least.

Before leaving we were greeted by a nice fellow, dressed in his tie, asking us if everything was all right with our meal. He was young and a little nervous but sincere. His inquiry was not in the least bit perfunctory in manner, which has often caused me to wince a little when hearing it in so many other establishments. He acted like a good host, made me feel like a welcomed guest, and seemed to care about customer satisfaction. Everything seemed to connect here. This was a special place, and I could not help but feel good about choosing this restaurant and enjoying a pleasant lunch.

When someone has been in the food service industry for what seems like a lifetime, he or she has a tendency to be critical and, to a point, cynical after walking through countless operations. When something is well done, especially in almost every respect, it is a joy to behold. One thinks, "Yes, it is possible to do things right, because someone took the time and cared enough to make it right." The true explanation as to why the operation I described exceeded expectations was that the leader who was directing this operation had put into practice what good management is all about.

The person in charge was obviously a professional who clearly understood the role of management and the key goals that had to be achieved. The primary focus in this operation was evident. It was to direct an extraordinary group of well-trained employees to perform their assigned tasks with skill and careful attention to every detail. This is the function and the purpose of teamwork and the essence of quality food service management. Everybody was in accord, directing energy toward satisfying customers. This was the goal, and everyone succeeded.

Excellent results do not come about automatically. Someone has to first set the ideas in place and make things happen. The individual manager must plan, organize, and direct employees to perform a service desired by customers. If those fickle customers become difficult to deal with or become disloyal, it is management's challenge to overcome. A manager is a leader whose main job is to train employees well so they can do their best. This can be done only by making each employee an important part of the operation. If not, an enterprise will suffer without everyone's full contribution. It is crucial for management to realize this concept and to provide a working atmosphere for employees that promotes the importance of maximum team effort. Sincere appreciation for good work is an absolute must if employees are to be motivated to do their best. It cannot be faked for the purpose of manipulation, for sooner or later a manager's convictions about people will reveal his or her true colors.

Some managers do not share this philosophy and have a low regard for hourly workers. I will never forget an incident that happened during an introduction to my first major assignment. I was replacing another manager who was leaving the company, and I asked him how he assessed the employees. I was interested in where the strengths and the weaknesses were so I could direct my attention accordingly. He responded, saying he considered them "the scum of the earth" and did not say another word about it. His harsh comment was so unexpected that it left me speechless. If I had been more seasoned at the time, perhaps I would have been able to give him back a stern retort. Though my experience in managing people was limited at the time, I knew this could not be right.

After he left and I began my tenure as the director, I decided that my approach toward my new employees would never be with such a negative attitude. As I got to know them better and began to share my ideas about quality and service, I found them to be quite responsive and willing to cooperate. Perhaps they were more amenable because no one had paid much personal attention to them before. This positive relationship continued to build, and over time our operation was the recipient of several awards for profitability and customer satisfaction. This whole idea about believing and working closely with the employees seemed to be working quite well.

I have never since been disappointed, neither do I regret believing in this fundamental principle. I continue to advocate this particular belief about people to be one of the most important foundations for long-term business success. There will be disappointments, and some employees do not belong on the payroll for one reason or another. Many times, it is nothing bad about the person but something in their personality type, past experience, or unique qualifications that just does not fit well for a particular job. If possible, a transfer to another assignment can be helpful in retaining an employee who may still turn out to be an outstanding performer. Helping someone find a job that is more suitable to his or her level of skill and ability can be one of the best favors you can do for a person, and a mature manager will readily assume this obligation knowing it is the right thing to do.

There comes a time when every manager must decide, for the good of the business, to terminate an unsatisfactory employee. Accepting poor performers and continuing to retain them reflects a serious management weakness. It is procrastinating and is costly to the business. Not only that, but it is unfair to the other employees who depend on the continued prosperity of the business for their livelihood. It is the job of management to act promptly. Terminations are difficult decisions that are sometimes nerve-wracking to make, but it is the responsibility of management to take the necessary action.

Making a change in managers is sometimes necessary as well, and it has far greater ramifications. It is uncanny how one simple change in the top position can completely alter the direction of a food service operation. I recall one particular example in which there was evident dissatisfaction with the food services at one of our college accounts in the mid-South. Dissatisfaction with the food service developed into a major student demonstration and a subsequent boycott of the dining hall. This was a real revelation that quickly got the attention of the college administration and the food service company. We knew that our client would be perfectly justified in changing contractors if we did not correct the situation.

The usual problems with the food service were obvious: The food was poor, the service was slow and unfriendly, and the kitchen area was not kept clean. True, the manager was new to this particular assignment, but he had a good performance record up to this time. We thought it was simply a matter of adjusting to a new responsibility, and we decided that, with some additional staff support, the problems could be fixed. During the next four weeks, we brought in a dietitian, a chef, and several others to get things under control. All this attention did bring considerable improvement, but somehow it seemed rather forced and did not feel right. When the support staff gradually departed, the improved standards soon began receding to their former levels.

At this point, we had no other choice but to make a management change. A new, experienced manager came on board the following week and went right to work. Due to other commitments, our support staff was not available to assist. The replacement manager was virtually alone and saddled with the responsibility of fixing several problems. However, his successful record in similar operations gave us confidence that he would make the necessary improvements. After a brief time, returning for a follow-up review of the operation was like witnessing the difference between night and day. The food was excellent, the service friendly and efficient, the kitchen clean as a whistle, and the student body apparently satisfied with the service. It was a complete transformation led by a manager who quickly identified what needed to be done, dove into the task wholeheartedly, and challenged the employees to give their best effort. The leader set the standards for positive changes, and everyone followed.

Upon witnessing these significant improvements, we wondered why we did not think about replacing management long before and saving ourselves a lot of wasted time and grief. Perhaps we just did not realize how critical it is to have the right leader at the helm. All the other support staff and the extra supervision are nice to have, but they are secondary when it comes to the performance of the local on-site manager. Obviously, the previous manager was not well suited for this particular assignment.

In reviewing the person's background more carefully, we found his strong suit was in accounting, and he had performed satisfactorily as an assistant manager at one of our larger accounts. At the time, we assumed this person was a great candidate for promotion to a larger responsibility, and because we needed a manager at this unit right away, we hurriedly made the move. Later, to our disappointment, the move from an assistant's position to a full manager slot was a bigger step for this particular individual than we realized. It turned out to be a bad decision. We did not recognize that dealing with the all the responsibilities and functions of a comprehensive food service operation requires someone with more well-rounded expertise.

It takes a strong person who has extensive operational knowledge and who is endowed with good leadership skills. Our mistake was assigning someone who did not fulfill these overall requirements. Even though attempting to shore up a weak link was an admirable effort, it turned out to be a waste of time and expense. We also learned the hard way that it is not a good investment to keep pouring resources into situations that have little chance of turning around.

These decisions are difficult because we do not like to give up on people. However, it is the right thing to do and kinder to the individual to make assignments according to his or her skills and abilities. These are tough judgments to make about our management people because the outcomes have serious consequences. It does not matter if you are operating a small deli, a university dining service, or a five-star restaurant — it always comes down to the fundamentals. Without highly competent management directing the daily business activities at the local level, the right things will not happen.

The failure rate and unacceptable turnover in the food service industry is a strong indication that we as professionals have a long way to go. In recent years, the service sector has mushroomed far beyond our ability to attract and groom an adequate number of qualified management candidates. However, there has been significant progress as pay scales and working conditions have considerably improved. Seldom are 80-hour weeks the norm, though some diehards still regard long hours a basic requirement to make it in this business. It is an antiquated point of view and not an attractive incentive, especially for the more intelligent, career-minded individuals. Those are the people we should be going after. Management today believes more in working smart rather than working hard and understands it is the results, not a lot of activity, that counts the most.

The image of food service as a profession has fortunately been elevated in recent years to a higher level and is no longer regarded as second rate. A lot of this is because food service, now more than ever, is big business. There are major players involved with big investments, and they expect big returns. Therefore, demand for professional managers is greater than ever and should continue to improve in the future. It is a wonderful profession, and if you are willing to learn, it can be very rewarding.

A number of years ago, I engaged in a discussion with another food service manager as to who was more important to a food service operation, a good manager or a good chef. I took the position of debating in favor of the chef since I believed the quality of the food was the primary reason people came to any restaurant. My opponent argued for the importance of the manager, extolling the practical truism that nothing begins or ends well in business without sound leadership. His conclusive point was that a good manager should be capable of finding a good chef or, for that matter, any of the other necessary workers. His logic in favor of the manager's premier importance was apparent so I conceded the debate, and I am glad I did. It was a good lesson to learn and has served me well over the years. This idea may not go over well with certain chefs, who sometimes think the manager plays only a secondary role. This may be true in certain situations, in which the chef with experience and management knowledge has been given the primary responsibility. Moreover, in cases in which the chef is also the owner of the business, he or she will readily admit the time spent in the management role far exceeds time with the cooking duties. In essence, they are truly managers. However, the title of "Chef" does carry a nice image.

If you like an ever-changing scene and can keep cool while everyone else appears to be enveloped in chaos, a career in food service could be perfect. You do not have to be crazy, but it helps. What this term "crazy" really means is that you must enjoy working where there is a lot of action going on. Managing the many complexities of a food service operation requires the ability to keep several balls in the air at the same time while remaining focused on achieving financial goals. You must always remember it is still like any other business in that it can survive only by making money. What makes it particularly challenging is that the objectives in the past, as well as in the future, depend more on people than on machines. Food service remains one of the few industries in which technology has provided only minimal advancements. You still must rely on people serving people. The public does not seem to respond well to being served by robots. It remains a personal affair, and that makes it unique and a lot more fun. The manager is on center stage, the main player with an unlimited opportunity for personal creativity. This special capability is apropos for serving a public that desires variety and numerous choices. The fundamentals of food service never change, and what makes it interesting for the manager is the flexibility to be creative and to convey service in his or her own unique style.

Chapter 16

Time Management — Practical Applications

(Getting control of the busiest of vocations.)

The saying "You don't have to be crazy to work in this business, but it helps" is a way to joke about the pressures of working in food service and to gain some momentary relief from the stress by using a little humor. Mostly it refers to the chaos that seems to reign in kitchens and dining rooms when employees are stretched to the limit. The hours are long, and ultimately fatigue takes a heavy toll on the best. People desperately want to succeed, but it is difficult to find the time to do all the things this business demands.

No one wants to admit it, but problems are often created by one's own doing. Getting the most important aspects of a job done well requires getting your business and your life under control, but more important, it is about managing time. It will not happen by itself. You must set priorities and get organized in your own special way. The key to solving this problem is having a plan and the discipline to stick with it. You need a personal road map with a clear list of the most important tasks to accomplish. The discipline required to stick with a plan is much harder, particularly in the food service field where issues and urgencies are constant interruptions. It is a question of how to find time to drain the swamp when we are up to our elbows in alligators. Such is the dilemma of working in this business, and it is exactly what happens when you gravitate to the things you like to do or keep tying yourself down to what is currently expedient. These activities can be major time wasters, robbing you of the time and energy needed to accomplish what is important.

A critical element of time management is first determining what is most vital for the manager to get done and then mustering the determination to delegate the rest. Like practicing self-discipline, it is not easy to do, and unfortunately everyone at some time or other tends to take the path of least resistance and do the opposite. The responsibilities of management require critical thinking, making hard decisions, and taking action. Thinking instead of busywork can be burdensome. Thomas Edison had it right: "Thinking is hard work, and that's the main reason why most people try to avoid it." However, to operate smarter rather than harder, it is the only real alternative.

Look at a three-step method to keep business and time under control.

NUMBER ONE: PROPER STAFFING FOR TIME CONTROL

Getting control of your time will be almost impossible until you have an adequately trained staff to run the day-to-day operation. To obtain and keep a good staff is a full-time job for management, and it is ongoing. A major drain on time is when employees do not show up or quit unexpectedly.

It is inevitable, so why not plan for it? Therefore, you need to be tapped into several personnel sources and have a pipeline of potential employees who are available. Being on the lookout and having a source of potential replacements will not only save time, but will also ensure better continuity for food services.

NUMBER TWO: BUILD RESPONSIBILITY IN OTHERS

It does not make sense to have a full staff unless its members are well trained and, most important, have essential responsibilities in the business. This is the foundation for time control, and delegating responsibility is a step beyond simply delegating tasks. It is first a matter of building trust so you can delegate segments of your business and not feel uncomfortable. For example, if you decide that only you can be trusted with the keys, then go ahead and be happy working 16 hours a day instead of 10.

To give the keys and some responsibility to someone else, you need internal control systems that will track finances. Of course, if you have not done the job of implementing a system of inventory cost controls, labor statistics, sales analysis, and budgetary guidelines, you are at considerable risk. Being without these control systems means you have no idea what is going on when you are not there. Once those required control procedures are in place, you then have an opportunity to delegate and have some peace of mind.

NUMBER THREE: COMMUNICATION ABOUT THE BUSINESS

Why some owners and managers fail to share vital information about where their business is going has always been a mystery to me. It must be some undefined fear or unwritten rule that employees should not know too much or it should not be any of their business. When you are an owner or a manager you have a vested interest in the business. That is what motivates people to work hard, take care of the details, and worry about what is going to happen next. Employees may not have as much at stake, but their job is their livelihood, and you must recognize that personal security is their concern as well.

They have an interest too, and they feel better about their jobs when they know about the safety of their employment. When management is willing to share vital information, most employees will take a more serious interest in the company. Of course, a certain amount of common sense should be exercised as to what information should be kept confidential and what is relevant. If you want employee cooperation and help with current problems and concerns, you must speak up and tell them. This is why regular employee meetings are so necessary. This is where feedback from customer surveys can take place and service problems resolved. Everyone becomes part of the solution and works as a team to make improvements.

Cost concerns, sales goals, portion control problems, excessive waste, correcting mistakes, and housekeeping are issues that employees need to know about. At the same time, positive aspects of the business should be reviewed, such as new sales incentives, reward programs, and some deserved employee recognition. Being open and concerned about people helps build an atmosphere of trust between employees and management. By keeping employees well informed and up to date you are setting the foundation for building a strong team and gaining their support for the times when you need it most.

Doing the most important things is easily derailed by the intrusion of those everyday unexpected urgencies. It makes life frustrating when you can't get to the things that are the most critical to get done. To keep priorities on track, some strong discipline is necessary to keep sticking to that plan. Busy management people need a focal point more than most. Otherwise, distractions have a way of drawing you away from paying attention to what should be your primary management responsibilities. Perhaps a personalized job description would be helpful. Post it at the work desk and include some brief words that highlight where your valuable time is most necessary and productive. Do not crowd your schedule too tightly, for some emergencies will ultimately require your attention. Leave yourself some wiggle room, and know that unexpected things take longer than you think. Though every situation has its own particular circumstances, a sample guideline of priorities for a manager could be as follows:

MY JOB AS A MANAGER IS TO:

- Provide direction and communicate daily with all employees.

- Recruit employees and provide a thorough orientation and training program.

- Build trust and a sense of purpose with all employees.

- Plan ahead to improve the quality and the efficiency of the operation.

- Analyze business data and take prompt corrective action.

- Be decisive and avoid procrastination.

- Report results to higher management on a timely basis.

- Meet and get to know customers.

- Continue to improve the image of my operation.

- Do something positive every week to enhance public relations.

- Spend some time on self-development and continuing education.

- Participate in a professional organization and network with peers.

- Be involved in at least one community service project every year.

- Balance time between work and my family.

The list points specifically to your primary duties and responsibilities as a manager and should in essence be your guideline for controlling time. Just trying to keep up with this list is enough to keep anyone busy at least 20 hours a day, but that is not the idea. You must do your best without punishing yourself. Striving for perfection will soon drain your energy and enthusiasm and make you a pain in the neck to work with. Realize that there will never be enough time to do everything, but you can manage a business well and retain control if you concentrate primarily on management functions. The point is that there is no time to waste. Filling in for untrained or frequently absent employees steals time away from your management duties. When that happens too often the business suffers, and achieving your true goals becomes even more difficult.

There certainly will be critical moments when you must step in to help production or service, but that should be the exception and not part of your daily routine. Managing a food service operation is a full-time job requiring all your time and attention. Performing tasks best done by employees, though perhaps satisfying to do at the time, just adds unnecessary hours to an already full workday.

Getting all the necessary things done may appear overwhelming, and as a business grows beyond your ability to control all the details, you must consider hiring an assistant. The person hired for this level of responsibility is of extreme importance and one of the most difficult decisions for a manager. It helps to review the aforementioned management priority list, for these are the responsibilities to share and to delegate. Doing it well and developing the new assistant will be a true test of your maturity and your management skills.

You must keep reminding yourself that the job as a manager is to get the daily work accomplished through others. There will be more time to manage where it is going to count the most if you concentrate on making your staff members more productive through daily coaching. It is not just the job they perform at hand but their ability and their willingness to think about what else needs to be done. The more seasoned employees understand this, and they go about doing a number of additional things that need attention without being told. It may be pre-prepping for the next meal or just helping out another employee who is getting behind. They see the big picture and how being prepared keeps the food services running smoothly.

One of the biggest complaints I have heard from managers about their employees is that they do not think. They always need to be reminded to complete jobs they continually overlook. They cannot see beyond their noses, they are unreliable, and they care only about their paycheck. What I suspect is going on here is a management attitude problem. The management does not expect much and consequently does not get much. It is a matter of personal belief about human nature. You either believe that employees want to excel, or you do not. Your employees may not have had all of life's breaks, but like everyone else they still want to improve their chances for the better things in life. They also believe in their self-worth and long for a sense of dignity. Take a chance, give them the benefit of your trust, and believe in their potential for excellence. Some will disappoint, but the rewards from those you have entrusted with responsibilities will far exceed the shortcomings of the few. This is how to develop star workers whom one day you will come to regard as indispensable to your business.

The ones you have built trust in will become loyal employees, and they will be the ones who will eventually allow you to control your time and life. This is a goal worth striving for, and smart managers will make it happen. Sometimes it amounts to reminding yourself that you are not the only person who has a brain. Have a little faith in employees; the results can be surprising. Give them your confidence and build on their self-worth. Most functions in the food service field simply require a person's common sense and careful attention to detail, and those who take pride in their work possess those basic attributes. Moreover, a person's best performance does not come about in a vacuum. Everyone needs a certain amount of reinforcement and some positive leadership. The kind of leader who inspires dedicated followers demonstrates a sincere trust, believes in worthiness, and builds upon a sense of pride.

Getting more done in less time can be a challenge, and for the most demanding tasks you need to function at your best. Determine your peak energy time, and schedule to work on the toughest jobs accordingly. You will get more done and usually get it done right the first time. Nothing is more time draining than having to do the same project twice. If you are a morning person, do not try to revise the menu program at 10 p.m. Some may ask how in the world they will find time in the morning when production requirements and deliveries demand their full attention. If you are a one-man show, you have no alternative, but if you carefully scrutinize your usual routine, it may be caused more by habit than predetermination. For those who at least have some semblance of a workforce, try to delegate something.

Avoiding those constant interruptions to preserve your sanity will sometimes require the taking of devious measures. You may have to escape and hide somewhere to avoid the telephone and all the people who feel they need you to solve their problems. Moving to an isolated spot to do your work and be free to concentrate is a necessity. My favorite location was always a corner of the dining room well away from the telephone and the center of activity. I was still visible and attainable in case of an emergency.

Having a bird's-eye view of the dining area also gave me some perspective of what my customers were seeing. It is amazing what you can overlook out front if you are always stuck in the back of the kitchen. Also, removing yourself for even a few moments every day to a quiet spot can provide a breather and help to recharge those overworked batteries. Taking some rest, though for brief periods, can be energizing and calming to the nerves. If you relish being in constant demand, then please yourself, but do not complain when you cannot find the time to get that revised menu pre-costed or your labor costs analyzed. When the staff learns to respect the boss's time, you will experience fewer interruptions, but you first have to set some ground rules. Let them know some of the things you need to do and why they are important. Also, having the confidence in your employees to handle some of the daily details without your constant supervision is a prerequisite.

Take a moment and give some thought to who is guilty of stealing time. Some of the everyday common ones to list are weak employees, turnover, a messy desk, salespeople, chatty managers, and anybody who talks too much. Help those who require attention get to the point. Train them to think first and then ask the question. Often, with a little effort, they can solve their own problems. Never hesitate to listen and to respond courteously to an employee who comes to you with a concern. Find out exactly what it is and how to assist. Just be aware of those who feel they should consume their boss's time so they can make an impression and be remembered. Explain to these talkers just how they will be remembered, that wasting the boss's time does not help when it come to pay raises.

For some, it is just a means of killing time and avoiding the work that needs to be done. Sales people who call without an appointment love to use up time trying to make a sale. Sometimes you buy something just to get rid of them. Prevent these intrusions by establishing a policy when and where you will receive sales calls and stick with it. You are within your rights to be assertive about this matter. Practice diplomacy but be firm at the same time. People with any sense will respect those who place a high value on time.

Alas, the paperwork must be done, or the job is never finished. Though a primary necessity for every business, if you let the paper flow get out of control, you can literally bury yourself in it. It can become so time-consuming that a business can slip away while you are nailed to the desk. I have seen this happen too often. It bears repeating that the action and the profits are not made in the office. The paperwork, or the profit and loss reports, will tell only what happened yesterday. That is important, but if today the deliveries are not being checked in accurately, the production is weak, or customer service is lacking, tomorrow's report will be just as dismal, if not worse. It is a sure thing when profits are not attained that higher management will be expecting even more time-consuming paperwork.

Reports will be demanded by superiors requiring detailed explanations of operating deficiencies along with a written plan of action. More time is then required for paperwork and less time devoted to the daily operation that ultimately is a reflection of actual performance in profit and loss reports. It becomes a no-win situation, and such is the dilemma. What you must realize is that there is a difference between doing paperwork and having control over the paperwork. Here again is a management problem about time. Every business of consequence requires a lot of paperwork, and if managers think they alone should do all of it themselves, they are making a big mistake. They must, however, understand it and have in place an internal balance and control system.

This means delegating the time-consuming functions of filling out forms, posting, filing, answering the phone, and responding to innumerable questions. Those are the most time-consuming office jobs and not the ones for a manager to get tied down to. There is a difference between trying to control all the paperwork and having the right systems in place to allow control. It is a matter of not combining the functions of posting records and making the bank deposits. The person who writes the checks should not be balancing the checkbook. That is called abdication, not a delegation of duties, so there is a control system of balance and cross-checking. A separation of bookkeeping functions is the key to effective internal controls to assure that someone does not have the opportunity to rip you off.

Do not be fooled by appearances. That honest face you rely on to take care of the office work may be planning to run off with the best day's receipts. If you allow opportunity and temptation to function because of a lack of implementing the proper control procedures, you can consider yourself just as guilty as the thief. The cash register was invented for a reason: to keep people honest. Now, with today's computers and test-proven systems available on the market, there is no reason for any food service manager to be without a good internal control system. That applies to all elements of a business, from the back of the house to the wait staff. It would be a major mistake not to make an investment in a reliable program and thus put the business at serious risk. A good internal control system will not only give you peace of mind, but will also save the management time so desperately needed.

Another time-waster is procrastination. Everyone does it to some degree, because at the time we do not feel up to dealing with the issue at hand. People do not realize that they have just lost a time-saving opportunity. Unfortunately, when they put something off for later, people have to deal with it twice, or even more. The main reason for this failing is a reluctance to make decisions, and one of the attributes of a good manager is the ability to make decisions. Often decisions have to be made when not all the information is available or may never be entirely known. This is where judgment based on experience and clear thinking comes into play. To get better control over time, make the best decision possible based on the information currently available. Certainly some of the more serious problems will require more time to investigate before coming to a proper decision, but 90 percent of all matters can be decided on sooner rather than later and the required action can be taken that day.

Take care of business and try to fight off procrastination as much as possible.

Those decision delays have a way of multiplying and will drain your time and energy. It might help if a sign reading "Do It Now" is written in big letters, framed, and put in full view of every manager.

Finally, when excessive time pressures get you down, you become an irritable bore and difficult to deal with. Think of how that affects employees and, worse yet, the customers. Whenever you begin to wonder why business is down or some employees are leaving, check yourself in the mirror. It started out wide on that first day when you opened the doors for business, but now excessive time-wasters on the job and the resulting fatigue have taken their toll. A once bubbly and optimistic spirit has turned a little sour, and so has business. Take a break and rethink how to manage a business and how to best manage your time. Do it now and get back on track.

Chapter 17

Food Quality

(Make it your passion. Even better, make it everyone's passion.)

One of the oldest maxims, "You get what you pay for," does not always hold true in the food service business. The experience can be a real letdown and proof that price does not necessarily always equate with excellence. At one time, dining out was a special occasion, but in today's busy, two-income society, it has become more of a routine necessity. Since modern life has exposed everyone to frequent meals away from home, expectations have been, to some extent, compromised and sadly lowered. People have come to accept mediocrity as a fact of life since there is so much of it, and everyone to some extent has had to put up with it. However, over time, the public serves justice on those establishments that do not pay attention to quality. People stop frequenting places that deliver poor or inconsistent quality food and service, and the business eventually goes belly up.

Go into a food service establishment at what should be its peak time and notice if the place is busy. If there are a lot of empty tables this should be your first clue. Beware: people are avoiding eating there for good reason; maybe the quality is not good. When a place is busy, it is hopping with energy, and when you must wait for a table, it is a good sign that the food is outstanding. One of the positive factors at work here is that a busy food service is turning over the food rather rapidly, and therefore the food being processed is fresher. It is not being held back. There is a heavy demand on the kitchen for food production, and there is a rush to serve waiting customers. This pressure automatically moves the prepared food along quicker, coming straight from the kitchen stoves, grills, and fryers. Most busy kitchens have an assistant manager called an expeditor who coordinates the quick delivery of plated food to the customers. If expeditors have a passion for quality, they clearly understand the limited time they have to work with to ensure food is served at its peak. Paying attention to serving high-quality food attracts customers — and lots of them.

It is worth waiting for a table in these popular establishments, and price is usually not the main raison d'être why people come. Customers naturally choose to be there because they look forward to enjoying great food, and through hard work and attention to quality, you keep earning their repeat patronage. Professionals undertake this responsibility with a passion and set the same high standards for all employees. They believe it is everyone's job to see that every customer goes away satisfied, and excuses are not tolerated. All keep their eyes open and sees to it that nothing that looks substandard in any way is allowed to be served. Quality control is in the domain of every employee, so mistakes are corrected on the spot. No one has to wait for a manager to make a decision as to whether something should be served or not.

This policy, to work, is a risk that management must be willing to take, and it is not a responsibility that is delegated easily. Employees must first be trained carefully on what exactly constitutes a quality standard. Some food services plate up examples of what a serving should look like, and some have color photographs prominently displayed. The important rule is that management does not give up after one or two training sessions. It has to be part of a regular schedule of review so it becomes second nature and generates a sense of confidence among the staff. New employees are given extra attention to ensure they are well prepared to make quality decisions. When it becomes a personal issue, then it is natural for employees to be more careful in handling their respective tasks. It becomes a built-in mindset, and mistakes are minimized. Less supervision is required because people do not have to be told every minute what is right — they know. When this philosophy exists collectively among the employees, you are fortunate, and the food service enterprise is on the high road to success.

Food quality means different things to many people, though most would agree it requires using only quality ingredients, preparation by expert hands, and the following of a good recipe. However, in spite of all the best techniques, if the prepared food is not served promptly and at the correct temperature, all the effort and expense that went into the preparation will have gone to waste simply because lukewarm food does not taste good. That is why great cooks without an effective delivery system do not make a go of it in the restaurant business. Without a coordinated system to assure timely service to preserve food quality, the best of creations can fall flat. This is where professional food service management comes into play, because maintaining quality relies heavily on the techniques of controlling temperature and good timing. It is a mixture of science and chemistry, cause and effect.

All foods, especially hot ones, reach their peak of perfection when they are cooked at the proper temperature and to the right degree of doneness. This peak does not last long, so timely delivery to the customer is of critical importance. If this is done proficiently you will be serving food of the best quality, which will be greatly enjoyed by the customer. This applies at every level of food service, from fast food operations to fine dining establishments. There are no exceptions to the basic rules of temperature and timing. The best prime steak in the world becomes third rate when served a little late, a little dry, and a little cold. A fresh hamburger properly served right off the grill is a lot more satisfying.

Here are a few basic fundamentals relating to quality control that every food service manager should understand and put into practice. When the following 20 operating standards are applied correctly, they will help produce a quality outcome.

1. China plates should be pre-warmed for plating hot foods and pre-chilled for serving salads to prevent proper food temperatures from becoming quickly drained.

2. Low-temperature roasting of meats minimizes shrinkage and retains natural juices. Avoid guesswork by using a good meat thermometer to produce the desired internal temperature.

3. Maintain slow simmering, not boiling, for stews and stocks to develop flavors and to maximize yields.

4. Maintain cooking oils in fat fryers at the correct temperature for the product, usually not over 350 degrees. Avoid overloading fryer baskets, which lowers the oil temperature and causes the excessive oil absorption that creates a greasy product.

5. Preheat cafeteria wells before filling them with panned foods from the kitchen.

6. Do not overload serving pans so hot foods become chilled or cold foods rise above safe temperatures. Replenish pans with entirely new, fresh pans when they are half used. Rework, reheat, and re-pan in the kitchen to maintain a quality presentation for the customer.

7. Cover food items during slow service periods.

8. Cook all foods, other than stews, soups, and casseroles, in small batches and prepare progressively during the service period to maintain peak freshness and to minimize overproduction. This applies to grilled and fried items, especially vegetables.

9. Produce egg dishes, pancakes, and other fast breakfast items to order. Prepare in sight of the customer in the dining area or the serving line whenever possible.

10. Prepare coffee in small batches. Keep it hot and replenish often to maintain freshness.

11. Use heat lamps where necessary to hold food temperatures, but keep holding period to a minimum. Too long and lamps will continue to cook and dry out the food.

12. Portion cake and pie servings only when ordered, to preserve freshness and appeal.

13. Purchase produce frequently and in small amounts to maximize freshness. Keep rotating daily; first in should be first out.

14. Do not overload refrigerators. Adequate circulation is required to keep foods properly chilled, and arranging neatly reduces the extra time that comes when searching for quickly needed items. Additionally, some things get lost and grow moldy, and that is money thrown in the trash.

15. Maintain refrigeration and freezer equipment in good working order. Provide thermometers in each, and check daily.

16. Ensure the automatic dishwashing equipment maintains wash water at 140 degrees and a final rinse temperature of 180 degrees.

17. Preplan production requirements for each meal in advance based on expected demand. Communicate effectively during daily production meetings with employees, and post a written copy in the kitchen.

18. Pre-prep recipe ingredients in advance to expedite production during the period of service. Retain freshness by keeping ingredients covered and adequately chilled.

19. Cover and return all leftover foods to refrigeration as soon as possible after each meal period. Use them or throw them away within two days.

20. Maintain complete production and service records to assist in more accurate future planning.

Many more food production quality control factors can be added to the above list that will apply in special circumstances. Those will come with experience and what you add to that knowledge through association with other food service professionals. The important thing is to have them become a part of your everyday practice. Above all, instill these and other high quality standards in the minds of employees, and make quality control an easy habit for everyone.

Quality is about who you are, your standards, and how you perceive yourself. It can be learned, but for some it takes longer than others. It is learned more by example than from someone's proclamations. Achieving quality food service is more about what is done, not what is said. It must be practiced and adhered to under all circumstances. Do not resort to shortcuts when under time pressures. The true test will come when you are under fire, for if you believe in quality, you will not allow yourself to be compromised.

Chapter 18

How to Hire a New Manager

(The one element you cannot afford to ignore.)

At some time in your career, as you progress into positions of higher responsibility, you will find it necessary to go through the process of hiring a manager. This is the most difficult of tasks and involves a great deal of risk. Hiring a food service worker is one thing, for there is a specific job to perform, and it is relatively easy to evaluate performance. When hiring a manager it is an entirely different story.

First, you must realize the magnitude of the long-term results that a manager's position brings to the establishment. You are essentially assigning someone the authority to control, to a great degree, the ultimate outcome, profit, or loss of an operational department or unit of the business. A lot depends on how much discretion you delegate and to what extent you hold the manager responsible. What is most difficult to predict is how a manager's leadership will affect the performance of others. A good leader guides the employees in a team effort to serve and achieve the desired objectives. A poor leader does not direct people well and may not even have a good understanding of the mission.

The selection of the right individual is one of the most important decisions and is the determining factor of where a business is ultimately heading. A successful outcome depends primarily on the ability of the manager. A good deal of trust in your choice of a manager is required, because the scope of the manager's discretionary influence is more than meets the eye. So many decisions are made on a daily basis that ultimately affect the success of the business that it is almost impossible to keep track of a manager's performance and why or how he or she arrived at those decisions. The only reliable record of achievement you can rely on is the profit and loss statement. Those figures tell the true story but will not reveal exactly how they got there. It just proves that more right decisions were made than wrong decisions when it comes to the bottom line. A good manager proves his or her worth by the consistency of achieving those profitable results. But there is more to it than that.

It is essential to clearly define what a manager is expected to do. Above all, a manager must be able to lead and direct others in accomplishing a multitude of functions in a joint effort to achieve preset goals and objectives. The manager must be knowledgeable in a number of food service disciplines though not necessarily an expert in any. Most important is a manager's ability to accomplish a high number of interrelated tasks through others. Though you can measure management success by the results achieved — such as higher sales, greater profits, and higher participation — you must also ask at what cost? Are sanitation standards being met? Are good employees being turned off and quitting? Are customers given extra attention, and will they continue to come back if they are disappointed in the service? There is more to evaluating the effectiveness of a manager than just perusing the profit and loss statements. There has to be a balance so that certain goals are not achieved at the expense of others. Some of these are intangible, but they are just as important to the long-term success of the business. You therefore must know a lot more about the character of the person you are hiring as a manager to predict how this person is going to make decisions that can affect every facet of the organization. Managers make hundreds of decisions every day, and most are made alone. These decisions are something that you trust will be made with good judgment and in the best interest of the business.

Do not try to hire a manager on the cheap. Expect to make an investment in both time and expense to attract the best candidates possible. It is truly one of the most important business investments, and it should be approached in a deliberate manner. Your own attitude toward this responsibility will make a difference in whether recruiting efforts are successful or not. You can look at it as a positive or a negative. If you perceive the pool of qualified candidates as limited and feel as though all the good management people are taken, you have already decided to fail before even getting started. You must believe there are good people with fine management talent out there always looking to improve their career situation and have no doubt they might as well be working for you. Good people are always ready to better their situation, and that is the only way to look at it. They respond well to enthusiastic leaders who recruit with a positive outlook and who project confidence in their organizations. It is a serious business, and the best people out there are looking for serious opportunities. They want to work for organizations that have a vision for the future and that are willing to richly reward their best managers for taking them there.

At one point in my early career, I was interviewing with a prominent and growing company in the food service industry, and it was apparent they were anxious to hire a great number of new management people. However, the interviewer seemed rather bored with the procedure and lapsed into using some scurrilous language. It seemed as if he was trying to act like he was just one of the guys, or so he thought, to gain some kind of rapport with the candidates. He unwittingly did not enthuse anybody, and we were turned off by his vulgarity. His tasteless behavior reflected poorly on his company's image, and I decided right then this was not the type of organization for me. Here was another experience in which I learned a practical lesson. To hire quality people, you had better make the best impression on those you wish to hire. The good ones will be interviewing you at the same time you are interviewing them, even though it may not be recognized at the time. The best candidates have choices, too, so the courting process is a two-way street.

It is short-sighted when this most important duty of hiring a manager is delegated down the management line in most medium to large organizations. It is not that the job cannot be done well by subordinates, but, in my view, when going after the best candidates there is a narrow period in which to set the hook. The ones who can make the most powerful impression are the top people in an organization. These are leaders who are in the best position to communicate the vision about where the company is going in the future. It is they who need to participate at a key point during the management hiring process. Take advantage of executive trappings. The finely appointed office decorated with awards and certificates of achievement make a fine impression, and the best candidates who are invited in can be made to feel important. Take a few personal minutes and capture their imagination.

You want to attract the ambitious, the talented, and the ones who will be the future leaders of the business. If the fancy office is not available, make an alternate plan. I would not do it for every candidate, but if on the verge of deciding on a good one, take the opportunity to reserve a private lunch at a good restaurant, or conduct the interview in a hotel suite. The uninterrupted time will be to your advantage, and both parties can concentrate on the important decision at hand. Of course, busy executives have time limitations, and it is not expected for them to participate through the entire process. A member of the staff or the human resources department can certainly do the screening and some of the preliminary processing. The senior people who neglect to participate in this critical decision process may one day miss out because they were not willing to make the time. Just remember, a top candidate has other choices, and you never want a good one to get away because the competition made a better sales pitch.

To attract a good number of attractive management candidates requires two things: you must advertise and also have a good reputation in the market. Get them to the door through advertising, but project that extra perception as a dynamic and successful business to reel the best ones into the organization. A solid reputation for excellent compensation, demonstrated growth in the industry, and the opportunity for career advancement will be attractive to many people. If that is the case, applications should be coming even when you are not advertising for management candidates. If it seldom happens, you may need to take a hard look at the perceived reputation of your company in the industry.

You also need to get keyed up about the hiring process before the need to fill a position becomes known. The normal turnover rate in any business tells that, if you wait for positions to become available, your recruiting process is starting too late. The job of hiring good replacements takes time, and hurrying at the last minute can be costly. Done properly, it can provide smooth continuity for a department's operation and provide ample time for some thorough orientation. It is a mistake to believe that you are saving some money by waiting to the last minute. Hurriedly placing a manager not up to the job will cost dearly, and correcting that error can be frustrating, as well as time consuming. Larger organizations should be able to afford hiring a high-potential manager and placing them in a staff position until an opening is available. There are almost always projects at hand to keep a new talent challenged and productive. If well controlled, keeping someone in the wings can be a effective strategy. In any case, hiring good people is a year-round job that should be top priority in any vigorous organization that aspires to grow and succeed.

Predicting a candidate's future success for the position to be filled is difficult to determine accurately. Many candidates interview well, ask the right questions, have the right responses, and are on their best behavior. It is easy to become impressed by an articulate and well-groomed person who may inadvertently distract the interviewer from fulfilling the primary objective of hiring the right person for the job at hand. The important thing is to know exactly, in writing before the interview begins specifically, the skills and level of experience you need to employ. Because someone looks good at the time, do not try to force-fit the person into the job and wind up with a mismatch. Though the human resource gurus are capable of classifying numerous kinds of personalities, I believe there are three types of managers that every food service organization requires:

1. The aggressive self-starter with plenty of experience who can open up a new operation or turn around a problem account, but who at times may step on some toes.

2. The maintenance manager who is not going to set the world on fire, but is well organized, follows proven procedures, and works well with others.

3. The new, bright assistant manager with loads of enthusiasm who is eager to learn and ready to advance toward greater responsibility.

It is wise to have a balance of talent and experience so you can address different problems and challenges without management and the employees colliding with each other. An organization works best when people have diversified capabilities and mutual respect for each other and are willing to draw upon each other's strengths. Your job as the leader is to intelligently hire and put into place a management team that can fill those various roles.

During the interviewing process it is your responsibility to carefully evaluate the key qualifications of each candidate to reasonably predict successful performance on the job. This is difficult, but I think you have a better chance if the emphasis for selection is more heavily based on the leadership skills of the person rather than on his or her technical experience. A hiring manager may think raw ability is required right now, but ultimately it is the character makeup of the whole person that will prove to be the best value for business in the long run. Though desperate for instant results, do not overlook the impact a new management hire is going to have on the performance of employees. A leader's primary function and responsibility is getting the work done through others, and that is the attribute most required.

Here is a list of seven factors that make up the primary attributes of a professional manager. Take time when interviewing candidates to see how they measure up to the following standards:

HAVE A COMMITMENT TO SERVICE

A food service manager must have a built-in passion for service and must believe that the customer is the primary focus and purpose of the business. By example, a manager's enthusiasm and strong resolve will carry over and motivate others in an organization to act the same.

BE ABLE TO DEAL WELL WITH DIFFICULT PEOPLE

The food service business is demanding, and customers are necessarily on their own time, have their own agendas, and can easily become impatient. Employees can become stressed out during peak service periods when everything is going crazy at the same time. Everyone now and then can be difficult to deal with. The well-rounded manager understands it is often the situation and not the person who is difficult. A professional can put things into perspective calmly and knows how to deal with touchy situations.

TAKE FULL RESPONSIBILITY AND DO NOT MAKE EXCUSES

Someone who operates with a childish "it's not my fault" attitude is certainly no manager. Question your candidate carefully and determine if he or she leans toward dreaming up all kinds of reasons why things go wrong.

MAKE THINGS HAPPEN

Some people drive the train, some people ride the train, and some cannot even find the station. Get a leader who does not wait around to be told what to do. This type may be a little difficult to control at times, but you will not have to worry too much about things not getting done. Do the job of communicating the parameters of the job for the newly hired manager in the first place, and this will minimize the squabbles.

GOOD COMMUNICATION IS KEY

When referring to having good communication, I am not talking about being a smooth and articulate talker, but someone who has the skill to communicate effectively both upward and downward. It makes little sense if the corporate executives are impressed with fine words if, at the same time, the people on the front line who are interacting with customers become confused and uninspired. The company's mission statement was not intended just for the annual report but was meant to be a living act of everyday performance. A question or two of the candidate regarding how he or she intends to communicate those ideals and purposes to the hourly employees would be in order. The answers can be revealing as to a person's management attitude toward employees and can be a critical factor in evaluating one's true ability to inspire and lead.

HAVE A POSITIVE PHILOSOPHY ABOUT PEOPLE

This does not necessarily mean that only eternal optimists succeed, but having a positive attitude is highly important. Choosing from a selection of equally qualified candidates is difficult, but the deciding factor in this business should favor the person who has great enthusiasm and whose outgoing personality will inspire others to act the same way. More important is how a manager thinks about why people work. You can believe that people work only for the money and that they intend to do the least possible for the most pay, or you can believe that people find purpose and meaning in their work and, if given the right opportunity and support, will take pride in their responsibilities and return superior performance.

For the former, a manager will tend to be dictatorial and have tight controls over the employees. The manager who believes in the latter will allow more individuality and creativity while keeping controls to a minimum. This refers to the X style of management versus the Y style of management. Extremes of either style may not produce desired results, and often flexibility is required of a manager to accomplish certain objectives under different circumstances. Modern management subscribes to the more democratic and mutually supportive Y style that has proven to be more effective and appears to foster better working relationships. You must decide which style works best within your particular organization.

GOOD CHARACTER IS KEY

All the other factors can be superb, but hire a manager without good character and you are heading straight for trouble. A manager needs to be strong in character and possess the will to resist the many temptations ever present in the business environment. This can extend from the many varied forms of personal dishonesty to the undermining of relationships. An organization's morale and overall performance is negatively affected, and most often, the evidence is hidden from ready observation. By the time it is uncovered and corrected, considerable damage can be done. Hire someone with a good reputation and a history of good citizenship.

References should be pursued with diligence by those most experienced and at the highest level possible. This is not the time to entirely trust your gut, for there are rascals out there endowed with great charm who, at times, have cleverly deceived and made fools of us all.

What motivates a candidate to accept an offer of employment? First, realize the primary purpose of the person looking for a job or changing jobs is to improve his or her quality of life, support a family, or impress friends by earning more money. Everyone wants security, nice working conditions, and friendly coworkers, but the base requirement is still the money. The most ambitious and talented candidates want opportunity for advancement, and that also translates into more money. The motivational experts you read about place money further down the line as a motivational tool. Yet when managers are evaluated for performance, the primary judgment about their performance is how well they have produced for the bottom line. Everybody likes money and what it does, and this is why people work in the first place.

They say if people like what they do, they will eventually be a success in that particular endeavor and make a good living. I think sometimes it should be the other way around; if someone makes good money, he or she indeed seems to learn to like much what he or she is doing. Some people are altruistic and abhor the crass elements of greed and blind ambition for no other purpose than accumulating wealth. Perhaps they would be much happier pursuing a career in social services and stay away from the world of business. That is fine for them, but the rest of us are in business to increase our wealth and enjoy the good life. Therefore, if you are hiring someone to help you make more money for your business, then be fair about it, and treat them the same.

A final note on why you want to hire a top-quality manager in the first place. There have been many instances in which companies and institutions have made significant investments in building beautifully equipped new food service facilities. Money is spent for costly renovations and decor changes designed to keep up with the trends and to be more appealing to today's sophisticated customers. In addition, a great deal of time and effort may have gone into upgrading recipes, menus, and service concepts. These investments were made with the expectation of generating higher sales and profits. After all these expenditures, not to invest in the management personnel who will be responsible for operating the new enterprise is a serious error in judgment. It is sad, but on occasion when customers happen to witness a display of poor food and service so disappointing at the opening of a new or recently renovated business, they feel inclined never to return again.

How regrettable it is after all the investment, time, and effort, and then the result falls short of what customers expected because management was not up to the job. Was it thought that things just happen automatically? Perhaps they just wanted to save money and hired staffing on the cheap. The point is that, if you want to make a substantial investment in facilities, you must have equal commitment when considering the investment you should be making in your people, especially the manager.

Chapter 19

Getting Ahead

(Taking responsibility for your own success.)

Your first management job is a thrill. There is a sense of excitement to it like a first date or the feeling when you just bought your first car. But it is different now that you are part of the business world and you are in charge of a sizable operation with real responsibility for sales and profits. Employees look to you for direction and leadership. All those days of preparation, education, part-time jobs, and interviewing for the big one are finally paying off. You feel good about your success to date, and it is deserved. However, it is just the beginning. You surely have big aspirations for the future, and there is a long road ahead. Now is the time to give some serious thought to the most important things you need to do that will keep you headed on the right path.

First, be aware that your employer looks at things from a different perspective than you do. Company executives' jobs are more complex, and they have many more things and people to worry about. You have been hired for a purpose, one of which is to help your boss succeed. Knowing something about your boss's scope of responsibilities will give you a better idea as to what you need to do to become a valuable asset. You can easily find out by learning more about the organization's structure, the corporate mission, departmental objectives, and long-term goals. Try to concentrate on the big picture and not just on your own particular part of the world. Get to know the person you are working for. What is their background, positions held with the company, their criteria for judging performance, and what do they deem most important? Avoid getting too personal, and do not try to press busy people too hard by putting them through a series of tiresome questions. Always be courteous, and carefully select openings for communicating. By being patient and being a good listener, you will certainly find out soon enough what your boss stands for and for what he or she holds as most important.

You may not necessarily agree with every point of view, and try not to be too eager to counter with personal views. It is all right to keep an independent mind, and you certainly do not want to be a yes-person. Moreover, it is not a wise move to engage in any strong debates with your employer, especially during the early stages of employment. You may be able to earn that privilege as time goes on but only after you have proven yourself as an established manager. Perhaps by then your point of view may have changed or tempered to some degree through experiences on the job. The important thing is to keep an open mind and to see things from your superior's position. You can learn a great deal more by being a good student and patiently crafting your own understanding of what works and what does not as time goes on. Some things have to be done for the good of the business regardless of your point of view. You may be asked for an opinion about a matter, but it is up to the boss to make the final decision. Support your boss with a positive spirit, and recognize that there are other factors that you may be unaware of, due to your limited scope of the overall business, that require a particular course of action. Your attitude counts, and a smart boss will surely sense whether you are part of the team or not.

As you go forward, increasing experience will give you more of an appreciation for making difficult decisions. It is a good idea to start out by understanding where others are coming from, and as you go further in a career it will be your ability to read people well that will give you insight as to what makes them tick and why they do things a certain way. There needs to be a lot of open give and take and a cooperative spirit to keep an organization running on the right track, which is often referred to as teamwork. Just be aware that good communication with your boss is the first commandment for getting ahead. That means listening more than talking.

Most objectives in business focus on two main important issues: reaching financial goals and solving problems. Of course most problems that need to be addressed in operating a business ultimately relate in some way or another to making money.

All the good business practices that we aspire to and admire in theory are for naught if the enterprise is not profitable. You need to keep reminding yourself that, in spite of all the bureaucratic hurdles you have to jump through, it still remains the primary purpose of any business; if it does not, the business will soon cease to exist.

Over the course of your career, you will be working with a great many different kinds of people — some you will like and some you will not. A few will be downright odd and difficult to work with, and you may wonder why they are still on the payroll. The fact is they remain on the job because management is willing to put up with some of their idiosyncrasies because of the important contribution they make to the company. Do not summarily shut off those who may be a little strange and who are slow to warm up to new people. By making an effort to get to know them, you may find them responsive to you for taking an interest, and they might be motivated to share some of their valuable knowledge. Others, who may be quite easy to get along with, may not have that much intelligence to offer, and, by aligning yourself solely with the gang of "good fellows," you may be missing out on a good thing.

One of my former dining room managers, who was a perfectionist when it came to customer service, was also a terror when it came to the kitchen employees and the way she treated her wait staff. She was a difficult lady, brought up in the old-school standard of strict discipline. She was extremely demanding of her staff to do things correctly, and when the kitchen sent something to serve that was not up to her standards, she sent it right back. I can still see her marching into the kitchen and raising Cain. Diplomacy was not her forte, even though she was absolutely right when it came to food quality and service. We tried everything we could to make her mellower, but nothing seemed to work. Finally, I had to let her go, because her insensible behavior was creating too many personnel problems to deal with, and good employees were refusing to work with her. It was too bad for someone to be extraordinary in so many ways but be unable to work well with others. It was a case of perfectionism getting out of control. Think about that when you may someday become so overbearing and demanding that others will not be willing to cooperate with what you are trying to accomplish. Learn to sell yourself to your coworkers just as you do to your customers.

One of the major keys to getting ahead is the ability to manage an area of responsibility without the need for constant direction. By being resourceful and a self-starter, it demonstrates to higher management that you are self-motivated, and those who are reap the highest rewards. The higher echelon in most organizations has a limited view of the daily operational details and the many circumstances that you encounter every hour of the day. These people simply do not have the time to monitor your every move, and if you were micro-managed, you would not like it anyway. It is not that they do not care; it is because the areas they need to keep focusing on are on a completely different level. They pay you, the manager, to solve the daily problems and to handle the details within your scope of responsibility. The superiors surely must have outlined some objectives, and they expect results. Excuses are not well-received. The only valid yardstick for performance is whether you have achieved the financial objectives or not, and it is a measurement that is not subject to dispute. When you constantly fall behind in achieving profit goals, it sends a message that you are not getting the job done. Then most everything you do comes into question, and you will be asked for reports on how you intend to correct the problems. When it comes to making money you are either a hero or a zero. It may be a harsh way to look at it, but in reality it is the truest test of how well you can survive and get ahead in this highly competitive world.

In real terms it is how quickly you react to business problems. When the cost of goods increase, find ways to absorb them through menu changes and/or price increases, instead of reporting that rising costs are the excuse for not making it this month. When sales decline due to the season, the weather, or whatever, promptly reduce staffing accordingly. When you determine a certain employee is not performing well, you must correct his or her performance or, if necessary, replace the employee. Promptly taking the appropriate action to correct problems instead of reporting some handy excuse is the way to become recognized as a star manager.

Every day you operate, there will be circumstances that will eat away at the bottom line. It comes from all directions: the competition, service breakdowns, higher taxes, higher insurance rates, theft, and equipment breakdowns. You could well have any number of these included in the list of excuses, but to get ahead, never submit an excuse and leave it at that. Always address the problem head-on and do something about it now, not tomorrow. Take the necessary corrective action and report only on the plans that will get business back on target. Higher management hires people for a purpose and counts on them for results. That is why, in business, you must always be on the offensive with a business plan that anticipates hard times. With goals to reach, do not depend on business as usual, or it will result in disappointment. Stay focused and do the things that will lead the way there. Keep promoting sales, improve training and customer service, innovate, upgrade appearances, introduce new specials and programs, keep up enthusiasm, and sharpen your leadership skills. Management on the offensive can readily absorb the bumps in the road that will surely come, and often the payoff will be an unexpected extra profit dividend. Those happenings can make a lot of people happy with you. The good results will build your self-confidence because you did not allow events to take control of the outcome, rather you took control and made things happen. Use your imagination, maintain a high energy level, have fun, enjoy your success, and share it with others. Success breeds more success; it will be contagious and recognized by those who make the decisions about where and how far you are going in the future.

During my early days of management, one of my superiors who, in his own right, was successful, frequently remarked, "A manager who continually works beyond a reasonable workday into the night and on their scheduled days off may be a hard worker, but he or she is no manager." This sometimes flies in the face of what we have always been told. Work hard, make sacrifices, and do whatever it takes to be a success. There are certainly those times when it becomes necessary to go the extra mile, but the key word here is "constantly." The message should be clear: if a manager is not organized, does not plan ahead, does not hire good employees, does not train or delegate and perform any number of strictly management functions, then that manager will pay the price of long hours and an unhappy existence. The road to success may inadvertently turn into a failure.

Too many good people have unwittingly hurt themselves badly because they have forgotten what their true responsibilities were. Excessively long hours caused by doing what should be employee tasks does not allow adequate time for the important functions of management that never seem to get done. Some that do get done are not done well for good reason. It is hard to be at your best and think clearly when you are just plain tired.

This dilemma of dealing with long hours is particularly hard on the small entrepreneur who is just getting started. The risks are high and the cash flow is slim, but you are filled with enthusiasm and energy for this new enterprise and you think you can do it all. It is tough going, and there is no way to afford the extra cost of a cook's helper, who would be helpful for those peak crunches, or the utility person who takes care of all those miscellaneous jobs.

The small entrepreneur winds up doing these hourly jobs him- or herself at the beginning, then it becomes a habit, and sooner or later it begins to take its toll. Though noble, it is a common mistake, and it is highly detrimental to your business, your health, and to your well-being. Before getting into this situation, try to remember what the most important things are that only you can do to ensure the future success of a business. No matter what the size of the operation, the most critical factor resides at the top line of the operating statement — sales, of course. It should not be a mystery; higher revenues in any business can usually solve most problems. Those sticky problems assuredly need to be taken care of, but without sufficient top line income no matter what you do, even cutting costs to the bone, the business still will not make it.

Line operating managers who have a sense for marketing and continue to expand company sales as one of their highest priorities understand this and rightly command the most recognition and rewards. Do not think about sales belonging to a separate entity and being restricted to only the salespeople. In a growing and dynamic company, everyone is a salesperson, or everyone should at least think and act that way.

Be mindful of the fact that, as the new entrepreneur or manager, there are some things that only you can do. It may be to locate a new site, decide on dining decor, create the menu, determine prices, develop purchasing standards, select advertising, push promotions, hire employees, or deal with any of the other numerous details necessary to please customers through great service and personal attention. There are enough management duties crying for attention every day to keep any one industrious person quite busy.

In addition, when it comes time for customers to be served, management needs to stay loose and have the ability to cover the entire scope of the food service operation. If you are tied down by filling in at one specific station, you lose sight of what is happening and sacrifice control of customer service. A manager has to keep eyes open on many different parts by moving about, making sure all the production and service activities are moving in concert, and being free to react quickly to repair any breakdowns. Think about that when tempted to save a few dollars by doing what should be an employee task. Just put a pencil to it. What will attracting one new satisfied customer do for business when compared to plating meals in the kitchen during peak service hours? How does spending time developing next week's specials, analyzing food cost, or meeting with a customer compare with cleaning the floors and taking out the trash? In the real world, of course, there will be times when you will be stuck with these menial jobs. That is what you must do at a moment's notice when those unavoidable breakdowns occur and no one else is available. However, if they become routine, then the shame is on you for neglecting the most important responsibility. Never forget that your job is to manage, and the better you manage, the fewer breakdowns there will be.

Long ago my father told me, "Let the underlings do the work." At the time, I thought he meant only not to get my hands dirty and to remember my station. I felt it a rather haughty, undemocratic point of view, and little did I realize until much later that he was trying to send me a much deeper message. It was not that I was so much superior to the workers, but my job was to give my full time and energy acting on the things only a leader can and should do. Some will still advocate that you must prove yourself to employees. Pitch in on a regular basis to earn recognition as one of the guys. The idea is to never give someone else a job you are unwilling to do yourself. Do not fall for this misguided notion, because sooner or later you will find yourself doing a lot more employees' tasks and a lot less managerial work. There is nothing to prove, nor should there be. Along the way, the most important things you should have learned were about operating standards and quality control. As a manager, these lessons should have provided a background of knowledge and the self-confidence to direct others to produce likewise. At this point in your career, you are charged with the more difficult task of accomplishing the objectives of the business through a number of employees. Therefore, do not fall into the trap of working side by side with the employees. It is easy to do because to some degree it is a reprieve from the pressures of management, and it is sometimes fun. However, to earn true respect as an effective leader you must fill and act the role with a purpose. That is what you are paid to do, and to get anywhere, that is where you need to be.

To keep growing, be mindful of continuing education. There are many opportunities to take advantage of, and they do not necessarily have to include higher-degree work. In addition to what a company may offer — and certainly sign up for as many of those as time permits — you can also take any number of outside self-improvement seminars that are easily obtainable. Perhaps the company has a plan that will reimburse tuition expenses for management-type courses that they are not equipped to offer in house. These might include Dale Carnegie, which is helpful in polishing speaking skills (an important capability for those who wish to advance), and some excellent and relatively inexpensive one-day programs that stress single-subject matters, such as sales, action writing, interviewing skills, or other pertinent subjects for the field of management. Check with local educational institutions that are always offering good management programs over weekends and nights for the convenience of busy people.

In addition to learning something new or from a different angle, you will likely meet quite a few other ambitious people and may learn as much from associating with peers in the industry as you would from the course teachings. At the least, you will be gaining some new ideas on how you might solve some of your current problems.

It is this ever-increasing knowledge you will gain from these experiences, and the many contacts you will make will be of more value than you can possibly realize. By opening doors and meeting new people you will be able to build an extensive network of professional contacts from which many new and exciting careers are likely to spawn. During these events conduct yourself as a person who reflects enthusiasm for the profession and shows a sincere interest in others. Remembering names, asking for the opinion of others, and making follow-up contacts with fellow participants will provide benefits far beyond the cost of attendance. Those in the industry who are too busy to take the time or make the investment are unfortunately missing out on a career-building opportunity. Sole owners should take note, for they have just as much to gain, if not more, than company managers.

Those truly serious about getting ahead must pay attention to personal appearance, their speaking ability, and their writing skills. It is a matter of shaping a positive and success-oriented image for yourself. The practical reason is that few of your superiors will have the time to get to know the real you. They sometimes have no other way to decide who is going to be their next promotion other than from their perceptions. It may not be fair so it behooves you to keep in mind the kind of image you are presenting. You may be smarter, have more education, more experience, and have good numbers, but if the image is poor, chances fall to slim or none. If you aspire to advance to the next level, you must start dressing and acting like those who operate at the next level. Superiors choose those who are ready to go and those who do not need a lot of advice on appropriate grooming and how to properly conduct themselves. Those who do not make the effort are judged to be somewhat backward, careless, or thought too uncomfortable working with those positioned at higher levels. Start thinking ahead if being chosen for advancement is a top priority, and get your act together. It is not that easy for those at the top to make the right choice from a field of comparably talented young managers.

Being able to socialize in a meaningful way is a good way to meet people and make important contacts. Most professionals on the way up belong to at least one community organization in which they give of their time and talent. Educated and successful people have an obligation to give something back to their community through service and while doing so have an opportunity to practice and gain some excellent leadership skills. An outstanding organization to become affiliated with at the start of your career is the Junior Chamber of Commerce. It is a good way to prepare yourself for the future when you will need to take an active role in any one of the many senior community organizations. Service is almost always a situation where everybody wins. The value of building friendships and future contacts can never be underestimated, and participating in worthwhile community projects will help you develop into a well-rounded person. While you are doing all these things and if you can still find what little time there is left, learn how to play golf. It is a sport for a lifetime, and in business it is clearly where the money and the power reside. It is a brilliant device to combine business with pleasure.

On the subject of pleasure, be sure to make some firm ground rules for yourself at the beginning of your career. In this day when many attractive men and women are working closely together in the business world, it is easy for emotions to get out of control. If it is one of the maddening things that cannot be controlled and you cannot possibly live without the other person, a divorce is necessary. By a divorce I mean a separation for both parties involved from the same employment site. Nothing is more disruptive than the time lost to all the gossiping that will certainly permeate the office, of which the couple may be unaware. It undermines morale, and, over time, it is debilitating to the performance of the organization. If it happens, use good sense and learn to find a way out so it does not hurt two careers. If it ever occurs when one person is still legally attached to a spouse, there will be real trouble. This is a potential disaster that should be avoided at all costs, or a heavy price will be paid for these unfortunate dealings later on.

The opportunity to entertain by showing appreciation to customers, generating new sales, and building good will can be enjoyable experiences for a rising executive. It also carries with it a certain responsibility, and that is to exercise some self-control when it comes to social drinking. Alcohol should be treated with a great deal of respect, for it has brought misfortune to the unwary and has led to the downfall of some talented people in the industry. Without lecturing on the subject, all I can say is think. If you do so and you are a big enough person with the good sense to exercise self-discipline and to act with moderation, you will be all right.

Along with the responsibility of entertaining clients and customers, an executive's position will involve incurring travel costs, and you will have the privilege of using a company expense account. You will be entrusted with controlling a considerable amount of expenses that you must account for, and it is expected that you will handle this responsibility with prudence and honesty. Be strong of character and never compromise the trust that has been placed in you. It is not worth taking some small advantage because no one will know and claiming that everyone else does it. Some weak-minded managers have slipped, and those stupid mistakes have foolishly destroyed more than one promising career.

When higher management decides to promote a deserving candidate it also has the immediate problem of replacing this capable person in the job that he or she is vacating. This is especially true if the person selected for advancement holds a responsible position that is important to the company. More than one excellent person has been bypassed because a competent replacement was not available. It may not be fair, but that is the way things work sometimes. Therefore, to be potentially ready to go further up the line, you must start grooming someone to take your place. This does not necessarily mean getting ready a reliable assistant who happens to be convenient, but someone fully capable who can step into your shoes and take over the job with a high degree of proficiency. It will be a measure of your management skill to train someone to take over. If you have someone else do it, you may not like who is chosen and may lose the credit and perhaps some influence over your former department in the future.

This process should not start on the verge of promotion, but at the beginning of any new job. Start building an organization from the ground up and prepare for the future. In the meantime, your reward will be superior performance due to the high quality of your personnel, and exceptional results will not hurt. Another benefit will be the opportunity to take on some additional special assignments because you have seen fit to be well organized. In this fashion you will prove to have capabilities beyond your current position. Having a reputation for developing management talent in an organization is regarded as one of the most highly valued qualifications of a successful executive. If you are serious about getting ahead, you will be prepared. Be a high-performance star and keep attracting them.

Whatever your level in management, you must not let time pass you by. When things are running along smoothly, which is to your credit, it is easy to fall into a routine and become satisfied with the status quo. However, it is important to understand that nothing stays the same for long, and if you are not the instrument of change, someone else may do it instead. Take an active role and initiate changes for improving your area of responsibility, and there are always things that need to be improved. Never believe in the adage, "If it works, don't try to fix it." That philosophy has been the downfall of many a manager who thought that not making waves was the best route to success.

True success comes to those who use their imagination and who continue to innovate. The competition is out there every day trying to beat you, so there is no time to lose. Not all new ideas work the first time. Do not expect them to. But progress will not happen without them. If one new idea works out of three, you are way ahead of the game. Stay alert, check out the competition, stay abreast of new developments in the industry, be well read with updated trade publications, attend conferences, and continue to be curious. Mostly it takes personal enthusiasm and a love for this crazy business. If you have chosen right, the time will fly by, and you will never have a chance to be a clock watcher, except to find out how much time there is left to get things done.

"Keep your shoulder to the wheel" is a saying from America's early days, when pioneers needed to get their wagons out of the mud. From time to time, either a business or a personal career will also seem like it is stuck in the mud. There will be a setback, a decision gone wrong, a serious employee headache, or any number of problems to deal with, and you may feel as though the roof is caving in. This is not the time to panic and quit. It is the time to dig deep into your resources and to keep on plugging. Dealing well with adversity can be the source of your strength that will help to gird you for those even tougher times ahead. The strength needed will be there if you have set your sights on a goal worth reaching. If desire is strong enough, you will surely overcome whatever difficulties may come your way.

These are times when strength of will and the determination to persist is the only thing that makes the difference in winning or losing. I had asked a question of a college president several years back about how he always seemed to be on the top of his day, even though it appeared his world seemed to be highly stressful. He said that almost every month he would read at least one book or an article about people in history who successfully overcame great obstacles. He mentioned that there is an unlimited supply of writings to draw on that provide true examples of human courage and persistence when in the face of difficult circumstances. He was convinced that any person who pursues an important challenge sooner or later suffers to some degree from fear and discouragement. The path toward every goal is strewn with pitfalls and false turns. Being well-read about people who have overcome adversity provides you with many true-to-life examples of perseverance. Their endurance, their faith, and their persistence can give you the spirit needed to keep on going. Everyone needs a personal source of encouragement to draw upon when times are tough and it feels as if your world is falling apart. It is a good idea to have some kind safety net.

Keeping your business and personal life in balance is a major challenge during your hectic climb for success. Most people intrinsically know the right things to do, but being human, they sometimes lose their composure and fail to use good judgment due to frustration or fatigue, the latter being more of a factor than is realized. There are times in any business enterprise when the occasion requires an extraordinary expenditure of time and effort. However, by pushing continuously beyond reasonable limits, people expend a tremendous drain on their mental and emotional resources that soon must be replenished. If not, there may not be sufficient energy to maintain the presence of mind necessary to address daily problems with a sense of objectivity and good judgment. Keep things in perspective, and do not try to be a hero at such a terrible cost that you risk being a failure in your personal life.

Conclusion

(Keep on following your dream.)

The information and ideas set down in these writings are not just my own, but also include input from the countless number of food service people I have encountered and worked with over the years. I am indebted to many individuals who have helped me by sharing their wisdom and knowledge of what makes things work. I have tried to distill, from all of these experiences, some basic principles that I think are important to know and to put into practice. These, I believe, are sound guidelines that are fundamental for running a successful food service business. It has been a long process of pulling it all together, and I have enjoyed telling my story. I hope it will add to your knowledge and help you along the road to personal success.

This is a most wonderful and interesting occupation. There are so many different things about it, and of special value is the unique opportunity to express your individuality in your own way. Every day is a change and a challenge that should test your abilities to the limit. It will require you to have a number of skills other than just preparing and serving great food. You also need to know something about accounting, business law, chemistry, psychology, and, most of all, human nature. Managers succeed mostly because they are well-rounded, know how to solve problems, take an interest in others, and continue to learn from their mistakes.

The market is always changing, and those who stay alert to the current needs of their customers are able to keep one step ahead. Today we hear a lot of public concern about health and good nutrition. Some companies have been challenged about their super-sized portions and the high calorie content of their core menus. Those who can best respond with common sense and intelligently solve these problems will earn the consumers' confidence. There will be rewards for those who listen and care.

I hope I have provided some insights about the various aspects of food service and the importance of doing the right things as a manager. There is so much more to learn, and the learning process never ends. If you are true to your profession, you will continue to gain knowledge from multiple sources. One of the best is simply hands-on experience and working with a variety of people from different backgrounds. It takes time, patience, and an incurable amount of curiosity.

Running a successful business provides a great deal of personal satisfaction and offers some priceless intangible benefits as well. People who enjoy life like to celebrate special occasions, and they especially enjoy doing it by dining out. How could you not feel enthused when serving a happy anniversary celebration or someone's birthday party? People having a good time, laughing, and smiling in your establishment must certainly transfer some good feelings to you and your staff. These are the simple pleasures of life, and making people happy is practicing your profession at the highest level. You are not just serving excellent food, you are giving great hospitality!

Let us wrap up with some typical sayings expressed one time or another within this crazy business. Perhaps you have heard a few of these on a number of occasions:

"Why don't they listen? I've told them a thousand times."

"The delivery will be there at 7 o'clock sharp."

"Can I borrow $20 till payday?"

"And what have you done for me lately?"

Glossary

A

A LA CARTE Items are prepared to order, and each one is priced separately.

ACCOUNTANT A person skilled in keeping and adjusting financial records.

ACCOUNTS PAYABLE Money owed for purchases.

ACCOUNTS RECEIVABLE Money owed by the customers.

ACTUAL-PRICING METHOD All costs plus the desired profits are included to determine a menu selling price.

ADVERSE IMPACT Impact of employer practices that result in higher percentages of employees from minorities and other protected groups.

ADVERTISING Purchase of space, time, or printed matter for the purpose of increasing sales.

AFFIRMATIVE ACTION Steps to eliminate the present effects of past discrimination.

AGE DISCRIMINATION IN EMPLOYMENT ACT OF 1967 Protects individuals over 40 years old.

AMBIANCE Sounds, sights, smells, and attitude of an operation.

AMERICANS WITH DISABILITIES ACT (ADA) Prohibits discrimination against disabled persons.

ANNUAL Happening once in 12 months.

ANNUAL BONUS Monetary incentive tied to company profitability and designed to encourage continuous improvement in employee performance.

ANNUITY Promise of a definite payment for a specific period.

AP WEIGHT As-purchased weight.

APPLICATION FORM A form that, when filled out by a potential employee, gives information on education, prior work record and skills.

ARBITRATION Third-party intervention in which the arbitrator has the power to determine and dictate the terms.

AS PURCHASED (AP) Item as purchased or received from the supplier.

AS SERVED (AS) Weight, size, or condition of a product as served or sold after processing or cooking.

ASSESSOR Someone who estimates the value of property for the purpose of taxation.

ASSETS Anything of value; all property of a person, company or estate that can be used to pay debts.

AUTOMATION Automatic control of production by electronic devices.

B

BALANCE The amount that represents the difference between debit and credit sides of an account.

BALANCE SHEET Written statement that shows the financial condition of a person or business. Exhibits assets, liabilities or debts, profit and loss, and net worth.

BANK NOTE A note issued by a bank that must be paid back upon demand. Used as money.

BASELINE BUDGET Based on a past budget and adjusted for current conditions.

BASIC MARKETING MOVES Basic moves that an operation should use to increase its sales volume.

BATCH PREP RECIPE Lists prices per ingredient for a detailed recipe for the purpose of obtaining a total cost for one batch of a meal.

BATCHING Adjusting recipes for equipment or recipe size constraints.

BEGINNING INVENTORY The quantity and value of beverage and food products or operational supplies in stock at the beginning of an accounting period.

BEHAVIOR MODELING A training technique. Trainees are shown good management techniques by role-play or viewing a film. Trainees are then asked to play roles in a simulated situation, and supervisors give feedback.

BEHAVIORISTIC APPROACH TO CONTROL Control through workers' desire to perform for the best interests of the organization.

BENCHMARK JOB The job that is used to secure the employer's pay scale and around which other jobs are systematized in order of relative worth.

BENCHMARKING Analyzing operation features in comparison to the best of its competitors in the industry.

BENEFITS Indirect payments given to employees. These may include paid vacation time, pension, health and life insurance, education plans and/or rebates on company products.

BID SHEET A sheet that is used in comparing item prices from different vendors.

BLIND RECEIVING When there are no quantities or weights printed on packages. The receiver must count or weigh items.

BLOCK SCHEDULING Workers begin and end work at the same time on a specified shift.

BONA FIDE OCCUPATIONAL QUALIFICATION (BFOQ) Requirement that an employee be of a certain religion, sex, or national origin where this is reasonably necessary to the organization's normal operation. Specified by the 1964 Civil Rights Act.

BOTTLE MARK A label or ink stamp with information that identifies bottled products as company property.

BOTTOM-UP BUDGET Secondary employees prepare a budget and then send it to upper management for approval and combining.

BOUNCEBACK CERTIFICATE OR COUPON A coupon good for a product upon a return visit. The customer is "bounced back" to the business.

BREADING The process of placing an item in flour, egg wash (egg and milk), then bread crumbs before frying or baking.

BREAK-EVEN ANALYSIS A computative method used to find the sales amount needed for a food-service operation to break even.

BREAK-EVEN CHART A chart that shows the relationship between the volume of business and the sales income, expenditures and profits or losses.

BREAK-EVEN POINT The association between the amount of business and the resulting sales income, expenditures and profits or losses. When income and costs are equal.

BUDGET A plan for a specific period that estimates activity and income and determines expenses and other adjustments of funds. Planning the company's expenditures of money, time, etc.

BUDGET CALENDAR The dates/time that a budget should be finished.

BURNOUT Depletion of physical and mental capabilities usually caused by setting and attempting unrealistic goals.

BUSINESS INTERRUPTION INSURANCE Insurance that covers specific costs when a business cannot operate as is normal.

BUSINESS PLAN Defines the

business image, clarifies goals, calculates markets and competition and determines costs and capital needs.

BUTCHER AND YIELD TESTS Testing of products to determine usable amounts after preparation.

BY-PRODUCT Item or items that are made in the course of producing or preparing other items.

C

CALCULATE Compute or estimate an amount.

CALENDAR YEAR Consisting of 365 days. The period that begins on January 1 and ends on December 31.

CALL BRAND The brand (of a type of liquor) asked for by customers.

CALL DRINK A drink made with brand-name liquor.

CAPACITY The volume limit.

CAPACITY MANAGEMENT The use of an operation's resources to serve the greatest number of guests.

CAPITAL Financial assets.

CAPITAL ACCUMULATION PROGRAMS Long-term incentives. Plans include stock options, stock appreciation rights, performance achievement plans, restricted stock plans, phantom stock plans and book value plans.

CAPITAL BUDGET Equipment, building, and other fixed assets.

CARRYOVER Amount left over.

CASE STUDY METHOD Method in which the manager is given a written description of an organizational problem to diagnose and solve.

CASH BUDGET The amount of money received, the amount of money disbursed, and the resulting cash position.

CASH FLOW Profit plus depreciation allowances.

CASH ON DELIVERY (COD) Merchandise must be paid for on delivery or prior to delivery.

CASH OR CASH OUTLAY FOR PROJECT Annual net

income (or savings) from project before depreciation but after taxes.

CASHBOOK A book containing records of all income and expenses of a business operation.

CELSIUS A unit used to measure temperature in the metric system, divided into 100 equal parts called degrees; previously called centigrade.

CENTIGRADE See Celsius.

CENTIMETER One hundredth part of a meter.

CENTRAL TENDENCY The disposition to rate all employees the same way, such as rating them all average.

CERTIFICATE Authorizing document issued by a bank indicating that a specific amount of money is set aside and not subject to withdrawal except on surrender of the certificate.

CHAIN OF COMMAND A top authority and a clear line of authority from that top to each person in the organization. Also called the scalar principle.

CIPHER Zero.

CITATIONS SUMMONS Informs employers and employees of regulations and standards that have been violated.

CIVIL RIGHTS ACT Law that makes it illegal to discriminate in employment on the basis of race, color, religion, sex, or national origin.

CIVIL RIGHTS ACT OF 1991 (CRA 1991) Places the burden of proof back on employers and permits compensatory and punitive damages.

CLASSES Groupings of jobs based on a set of rules for each grouping. Classes usually contain similar jobs.

CLASSICAL PRINCIPLES (OR THEORY) OF ORGANIZATION Focuses on enterprise structure and work allocation.

CLASSIFICATION (OR GRADING) METHOD Categorizing jobs into groups.

CLASSIFICATION RANKING SYSTEM Constitutes grades and

categories to rank various jobs.

COLLECTIVE BARGAINING
Representatives of management and the union meet to negotiate the labor agreement.

COMMISSION An individual's pay based on the amount of sales personally derived.

COMMITTED ITEM A product that is scheduled for production between the time it is ordered and the time it is received.

COMMON SIZE ANALYSIS
Analysis of financial statements by dividing each item on two or more statements by the total revenue for the period.

COMPARATIVE ANALYSIS
Analysis of displaying the difference of line items on financial statements for two or more financial periods or two or more financial dates along with the percentage changes.

COMPENSABLE FACTOR
A fundamental, compensable element of a job, such as skills, effort, responsibility and working conditions.

COMPENSATION Something given in return for a service or a value.

COMPETITIVE ADVANTAGE
The elements that allow an organization to distinguish its product or service from those of its competitors.

COMPOUND Composed of more than one part.

COMPUTERIZED By means of a computer or computers.

CONFIGURATION An arrangement.

CONFRONTATION MEETINGS The method of explaining and bringing up intergroup misconceptions and problems so that they can be resolved.

CONSIGNMENT PRODUCTS
Items provided to a company by a vendor who charges for them after they are used.

CONSUMER ORIENTATION
The needs of consumers determine management decisions.

CONTRIBUTION RATE The contribution margin, in dollars, divided by sales.

CONTROL To have charge of.

COOK/CHILL SYSTEM Cooking food item to "almost done" state, packaging it (above pasteurization temperature) and chilling it rapidly.

CO-OP BUYING A group of similar operations working together to secure pricing through mass purchasing at quantity discount prices.

CORPORATION A group of people who obtain a charter giving them (as a group) certain legal rights and privileges distinct from those of the individual members of the group.

COST The amount paid to acquire or produce an item.

COST ALLOCATION The process of distributing costs among departments.

COST CONTROLLER The person or people whose responsibilities include analyzing expenses, revenues, and staffing levels.

COST FACTOR Cost calculated by dividing the cost per servable pound by the purchase price per pound.

COST LEADERSHIP Being the low-cost leader in an industry.

COST OF SALES Food and beverage cost for menu items in relation to the sales attained by these items during a specific period.

COST PER PORTION The cost of one serving calculated by total recipe cost divided by the number of portions.

COST PER SERVABLE POUND The cost calculated by multiplying the purchase price by the cost factor.

COST-BENEFIT ANALYSIS Determining the cost, in monetary terms, of producing a unit within a program.

COST-EFFECTIVENESS ANALYSIS Identifying the cost, in nonmonetary terms, of producing a unit.

COST-PLUS Paying vendors cost plus a percentage.

COUNT The number of units or items.

CPA (CERTIFIED PUBLIC ACCOUNTANT) An accountant

who has fulfilled certain requirements and abides to rules and regulations prescribed by the American Institute of Certified Public Accountants.

CPP (COST PER POINT) BUDGETING Method used to obtain an advertising level at a predetermined cost.

CRITERION VALIDITY Validity is based on showing that scores on a test are related to job performance.

CULTURAL CHANGE Changes in a company's shared values and aims.

CURRENT LIABILITY A debt or obligation that will become due within a year.

CURRENT RATIO Current assets divided by current liabilities.

CUTTING LOSS Weight lost from a product during fabrication.

CVP The relationship between cost, volume, and profit.

D

DAILY PRODUCTION REPORT A list of items and quantities produced during a specific shift or day.

DEAD STOCK ITEM Item no longer offered.

DEBIT Showing something owed or due.

DECAMETER Equal to 10 meters.

DECIMAL A system of counting by tens and powers of ten.

DECIMETER Equal to one tenth of a meter.

DEDUCTION A value that may be subtracted from taxable income.

DEFAULT Failure to pay when due.

DEFERRED PROFIT-SHARING PLAN A plan in which a certain amount of profits are credited to an employee's account. May be payable at retirement, termination or death.

DEFINED BENEFIT PENSION PLAN A formula for determining retirement benefits.

DEFINED-CONTRIBUTION

PLAN The employer makes specific contributions to an employee's pension but does not guarantee the amount.

DEGREE DAY The difference between outside temperature and 65° F.

DELEGATION Distribution of authority and responsibility downward in the chain of command.

DEMOGRAPHIC SEGMENTATION Segmentation based on human population variables such as age, gender, and family size.

DENOMINATOR Common trait or standard.

DEPOSIT To put in a place, especially a bank, for safekeeping.

DEPRECIATION Lessening or lowering in value.

DESIGNATE Point out; indicate definitely.

DIFFERENTIAL (BEVERAGE) Difference of the sales value of a drink from the standard sales value of beverages used.

DIFFERENTIATE To distinguish a product or service from similar products or services.

DIFFERENTIATION Trying to be unique within an industry with dimensions that are valued by buyers.

DIRECT COSTS (FOOD) The costs associated with direct purchases.

DIRECT ISSUE Items that are directly delivered and charged to a food-and-beverage outlet — not stored in a central storeroom.

DIRECT LABOR Labor used directly in the preparation of a food item.

DIRECT PURCHASES Food delivered directly into the kitchen and charged as a food cost on that day.

DIRECTING Showing and explaining to others what needs to be done and helping them do it.

DISCIPLINE A correction or action toward a subordinate when a rule or procedure has been violated.

DISMISSAL Involuntary termination of employment.

DIVIDEND An owner's share of the surplus when a company shows a profit at the end of a period.

DIVISOR A number by which another (the dividend) is divided.

DOWNSIZING The process of reducing the size of an operation.

E

EARNINGS PER SHARE Earnings of a company divided by the number of its stock shares outstanding.

EARNINGS RATIO The net profit before taxes divided by net sales.

ECONOMIC ORDER QUANTITY (EOQ) Determines a purchase quantity that does the best of minimizing purchases and inventory costs.

ECONOMIC STRIKE A strike resulting from a failure to agree about terms of a contract that involve wages, benefits, and other employment conditions.

EDIBLE PORTIONS (EP) The actual yield available for processing a food item.

ELASTICITY OF DEMAND How demand for a product can fluctuate in response to other factors.

ELASTICITY OF SUPPLY The response of output to changes in price. Quantity supplied divided by the percentage change in the price.

ELECTRONIC DATA INTERCHANGE (EDI) Allows a food-service operator to receive prices electronically and generate an order form to send back.

ELECTRONIC SPREADSHEET Computerized worksheet with vertical and horizontal columns that are easily manipulated.

EMBEZZLEMENT Taking of property by someone to whose care it has been entrusted.

EMPLOYEE ADVOCACY Human Resources takes responsibility for defining how management should treat employees and represents the interests of employees within the framework of its obligation to senior management.

EMPLOYEE ASSISTANCE PROGRAM (EAP) Program employers promote to help employees overcome a problem, usually in regard to alcoholism or drug abuse,

EMPLOYEE COMPENSATION Any form of pay or reward an employee gets from his or her employment.

EMPLOYEE ORIENTATION Introduction of basic company background information to new employees.

EMPLOYEE RETIREMENT INCOME SECURITY ACT (ERISA) The law that provides government protection of pensions for all employees with pension plans.

EMPLOYEE STOCK OWNERSHIP PLAN (ESOP) A company contributes shares of its own stock to a trust to which additional contributions are made annually. Upon retirement or separation from service the trust distributes the stock to employees.

EMPOWERMENT Giving lower-level employees the opportunity, responsibility, and authority to solve problems.

ENDING INVENTORY The quantity and value of items on hand at the end of a period.

ENTREE The main dish of a meal.

ENTROPY Lack of useful input causing a system to solidify or run down.

EP WEIGHT Edible portion weight. The usable portion after processing.

EQUAL EMPLOYMENT OPPORTUNITY COMMISSION (EEOC) The commission, created by Title VII, empowered to investigate job discrimination complaints and sue on behalf of complainants.

EQUAL PAY ACT OF 1963 An amendment to the Fair Labor Standards Act designed to require equal pay for women doing the same work as men.

EQUIPMENT Machines or major tools necessary to complete a given task.

EQUITY FINANCING Financing by owners of the organization or company.

EQUIVALENT Equal in value or power.

ESTIMATE Judgment or guess determining the size or value of an item.

EVALUATE To find the value or amount of.

EXCEPTION PRINCIPLE Recurring decisions are handled in the normal manner, and specific ones are referred upward for appropriate action.

EXPECTANCY CHART Shows the relationship between test scores and job performance.

EXPENDITURE Amount spent.

EXPIRATION The date on which a food or beverage product ceases to be usable.

EXPLODED RECIPE Changing recipe quantities to create the number of portions required.

EXTENSION To equate out, lengthen or widen.

EXTRA INDUSTRY Comparison of your practices with other industries.

F

FABRICATED Made or made up.

FABRICATED PRODUCT The item after trimming, boning, or portioning.

FABRICATED YIELD PERCENTAGE The yield, or edible portion, of an item shown as a percentage of the item as purchased.

FACTOR One of two or more quantities, multiplied.

FACTOR SYSTEM Raw food cost is multiplied by a factor to determine a menu selling price.

FAIR LABOR STANDARDS ACT Passed in 1936 to provide for minimum wages, maximum hours, overtime pay, and child labor protection.

FINANCES Funds, money or revenue; financial condition.

FINANCIAL POSITION The status of a company's assets, liabilities, and equity.

FINANCIAL STATEMENTS Used in a business operation to inform management of its exact financial position.

FINISHED GOODS Menu items that are prepared and ready to serve.

FIRM PRICE The price agreed to by the purchaser and vendor.

FISCAL YEAR The time between one yearly settlement of financial accounts and another.

FIXED BUDGET Budget figures based on a definite level of activity.

FIXED EMPLOYEES Employees who are necessary no matter the volume of business.

FLEX PLAN A plan giving employees choices regarding benefits.

FLEXIBLE BUDGET Projected revenue and expenditures based on production.

FLEXIBLE CAPACITY STRATEGY Handling varying volumes of business without having high overhead costs.

FLEXTIME A system that allows employees to build their workdays around a core of midday hours.

FLIGHT The period of an advertiser's campaign.

FLUCTUATE Change continually.

FOOD COST The cost of food items purchased for resale.

FOOD INGREDIENT DATABASE Contains basic information about each food item. Name, cost, purchase units, inventory units, issue units, vendors, and conversion factors are included.

FOOD ITEM DATA FILE (FIDF) NUMBER The number assigned to a food item in a database.

FOOD COST PERCENTAGE Cost of food divided by sales from that food.

FORECAST A prediction.

FORECASTING Estimating

future revenue and expense.

FORMAT Refers to size, shape, and general arrangement of a book or magazine.

FORMULA A recipe or equation.

FOUR Cs OF CREDIT Character, capital, collateral, and the capacity to repay.

FOUR-DAY WORKWEEK An arrangement that allows employees to work four ten-hour days instead of the more usual five eight-hour days.

FRACTION One or more of the equal parts of a whole.

FRANCHISE A franchise grants the right to use a name, methods and product in return for franchise fees.

FRANCHISEE The person or organization acquiring the franchise.

FRANCHISOR The person or company selling the franchise.

FREEZER BURN Fat under the surface of food having become rancid and possibly having caused a brown deterioration.

FTE, OR FULL-TIME EQUIVALENT A method of measuring labor costs with use of overtime pay.

FUNDAMENTAL EQUATION ASSETS Liabilities plus equity.

G

GARNISH To decorate.

GELATIN A tasteless, odorless substance that dissolves easily in hot water and is used in making jellied desserts and salads.

GENERAL LEDGER (GL) A ledger containing all financial statement accounts.

GOURMET A lover of fine foods.

GRADUATED Arranged in regular steps, stages, or degrees.

GRAM Twenty-eight grams are equal to one ounce.

GRATUITY / TIP A gift or money given in return for a service.

GRAZING When employees consume food, unauthorized.

GRIEVANCE A complaint against the employer which may include factors involving wages, hours, or conditions of employment.

GROSS The overall total.

GROSS COST The total cost of food consumed.

GROSS MARGIN Sales minus the cost of food.

GROSS PAY Money earned before deductions are subtracted.

H

HARD WATER Water containing excessive calcium and magnesium.

HEALTH MAINTENANCE ORGANIZATION (HMO) Health-care providers that use their own physicians and facilities.

HECTOMETER Equal to 100 meters.

HEDGING A contract on a future price entered into to secure a fixed price.

HOMOGENEOUS ASSIGNMENT A form of specialization that assigns an employee to one job or limits the employee to a related specific task.

HORIZONTALLY On the same level.

HOST/HOSTESS The person who receives guests.

HOUSE BRAND The brand of liquor normally served by a given bar.

HVAC Heating, ventilation, and air-conditioning.

HYPOTHETICAL Assumed or supposed.

I

IMPERIAL SYSTEM A measurement system using pounds and ounces for weights and pints for volume.

INDICATOR That which points out.

INGREDIENT One part of a mixture.

INGREDIENT ROOM Where non-cooking personnel prepare food before it is sent to cooking personnel.

INSTALLMENT Part of a sum of

money or debt to be paid at regular times.

INSUBORDINATION Willful disobedience or disregard of a boss's authority.

INSURANCE Trading the possibility of a loss for the certainty of reimbursement. Paid by small premiums.

INTEGRATED BEVERAGE CONTROL SYSTEM An automatic beverage dispensing system integrated with a computer or point-of-sale register.

INTEREST Money paid for the use of borrowed money.

INTERNAL CONTROL The methods and measures within a business to safeguard assets, check the accuracy and reliability of accounting data, and promote operational efficiency.

INVENTORY A list of items with their estimated value and the quantity of each.

INVENTORY CONTROL System used for maintaining inventories.

INVENTORY CONTROL METHOD (BEVERAGE) Method in which the beverage amount used is determined from guest checks and then reconciled with replacement requisitions.

INVENTORY TURNOVER The amount of times inventory turns over during a specific period.

INVENTORY VARIANCE ACCOUNTING The amount of sales of an item is compared with the number used from inventory records, and the variance is noted.

INVERT Turn upside down.

INVOICE Shows prices and amounts of goods sent to a purchaser.

ITEMIZE To state by item.

J

JIGGER Used to serve a predetermined volume of a beverage.

JOB ANALYSIS Job description and specifications.

JOB DESCRIPTION A description of tasks and duties required on a job.

JOB SHARING Allowing two or more people to share a single full-time job.

JOB SPECIFICATIONS The qualifications needed to hold a job. Includes educational, physical, mental, and age requirements.

K

KILOGRAM Equal to 1,000 grams.

KILOMETER Equal to 1,000 meters.

KLEPTOMANIA The persistent impulse to steal.

L

LAPPING A type of embezzlement when funds are taken from an account then covered with later receipts.

LEAST SQUARES ANALYSIS In-depth method of calculating an average of variable or fixed costs.

LEGUMES Vegetables, especially beans and peas; technically, plants in the pea family, or the fruits and seeds of such plants.

LEVERAGING Using borrowed money to acquire assets to make money.

LIABILITY Being under obligation or debt.

LINE MANAGER The manager who is authorized to direct work and is responsible for accomplishing the company's goals.

LINE OF IMPLEMENTATION Division of planning and organizing activities from "doing" activities.

LIQUIDITY RATIOS Ratios that show the ability to meet short-term obligations.

LIQUOR COST Amount paid for liquor after discounts.

LIQUOR COST PERCENT The portion cost divided by the selling price.

LITER Metric system measure of volume.

LOCKOUT When an employer refuses to provide opportunities to work.

LOGO Trademark.

LONG-TERM DEBT Fixed liabilities.

LOSS CONTROL Attempting to prevent losses.

M

MAITRE D' Person in charge of dining room service.

MANAGEMENT BY OBJECTIVES (MBO) Setting measurable goals with employees and periodically reviewing their progress.

MANAGEMENT PROCESS Five basic functions of planning, organizing, staffing, leading, and controlling.

MANAGEMENT PROFICIENCY RATIO Net profit after taxes divided by total assets.

MANUAL Done by hand.

MARGIN The difference between the cost and the selling price.

MARGINAL COST The amount of output by which aggregate costs are changed if the volume of output is increased or decreased by one unit.

MARKET Groups with similar characteristics, wants, needs, buying power and willingness to spend for dining or drinking out.

MARKET PRICE INDEX Used to show the change in the cost of raw foods.

MARKET SHARE The share of a market that a business has for its products or services.

MARKETING Means by which an outlet is exposed to the public.

MARKETING OBJECTIVES Measurable and achievable goals that marketing efforts are intended to accomplish.

MARKETING PERSPECTIVE Consumer satisfaction is placed first in all planning, objectives, policies, and operations.

MARKETING POLICY A course of action to be followed as long as conditions exist.

MARKETING SEGMENTATION Dividing the market into smaller sub-markets or segments.

MARKETING STRATEGY

Overall plan of action that enables the outlet to reach an objective.

MARKUP Amount by which a higher price is set.

MBWA Management by walking around.

MEASURE A lineal measure equal to a thousandth of a meter.

MEAT TAG Used for identification and verification.

MEDIA Various types of advertising, such as television, radio, and newspapers.

MEDIATION Intervention using a neutral third party to help reach an agreement.

MEDICARE A federal health insurance program for people 65 or older and certain disabled people.

MENU A list of dishes served at a meal.

MENU ENGINEERING Technique that is used for analyzing menu profitability and popularity.

MENU MIX Menu popularity calculation.

MENU PREFERENCE FORECASTING Predicts how various items will sell when in competition with other items.

MENU PRICE The amount that will be charged for an item.

METRIC Pertains to the meter or to the system of weights and measures based on the meter and the kilogram.

MILL When dealing with monetary numbers, the third place to the right of the decimal.

MILLIGRAM One thousandth part of a gram.

MILLILITER One thousandth part of a liter.

MILLIMETER One thousandth part of a meter.

MISSION STATEMENT A statement giving the reason why the organization exists and what makes it different from other organizations.

MODEM ORGANIZATION THEORY A behavioral approach to organization.

MODULE A discrete and identifiable program.

MONETARY To do with money or coinage.

MOVING AVERAGE The total of demand in previous periods divided by the number of periods.

MUNICIPAL SOLID WASTE (MSW) Waste products that are deposited in landfills.

N

NATIONAL EMERGENCY STRIKES Strikes that might "imperil the national health and safety."

NET The remaining amount after deducting all expenses.

NET PRESENT VALUE (NPV) The present value of future returns discounted at the appropriate cost of capital minus the cost of the investment.

NET PROFIT Profit after all product costs, operating expenses and promotional expenses have been deducted from net sales.

NET PURCHASE PRICE The price paid by the company for one unit.

NET WORTH Excess value of resources over liabilities.

NORRIS-LAGUARDIA ACT This law marked the era of strong encouragement of unions and guaranteed each employee the right to bargain collectively "free from interference, restraint, or coercion."

NUMERAL Symbol for a number.

O

OCCUPATIONAL MARKET CONDITIONS Published projections of labor supply and demand for various occupations by the Bureau of Labor Statistics of the U.S. Department of Labor.

OCCUPATIONAL SAFETY AND HEALTH ACT Law passed by Congress in 1970 assuring every working man and woman in the nation safe and healthful working conditions to preserve our human resources.

OCCUPATIONAL SAFETY AND HEALTH

ADMINISTRATION (OSHA) The agency created within the Department of Labor to set safety and health standards for all workers in the United States.

ON-THE-JOB TRAINING (OJT) Training to learn a job while working it.

OPEN BAR Practice at banquet functions whereby customers are not charged individually for the drinks they consume. The host pays for banquet-goers' consumption.

OPEN DEPARTMENT REGISTER KEYS Keys that break down sales by categories.

OPEN MARKET BUYING Food purchasing method where competitive bids are secured for various items.

OPERATING BUDGET Detailed revenue and expense plan for a determined period.

OPERATING RATIO Net profit divided by net sales.

ORGANIZATIONAL CHART Shows the relationships of jobs to each other with lines of authority, responsibility and communication.

ORGANIZATIONAL DEVELOPMENT INTERVENTIONS Techniques aimed at changing employees' attitudes, values, and behavior.

OUTPUT The end product.

OUTSOURCING Calling upon other companies help supply your products.

OVERHEAD-CONTRIBUTION METHOD All non-food cost percentages are subtracted from 100. The resulting figure is divided into 100, and that figure times the raw food cost equals the menu selling price.

OVERTIME Time exceeding regular hours.

P

P AND L SHEET A profit and loss statement.

PAR STOCK Stock levels established by management for individual inventory items in varying locations.

PARKINSON'S LAW Workers

adjust pace to the work available.

PAYBACK PERIOD Period of time required to recover an expenditure.

PAYROLL A list of employees and amounts to pay them, as well as records pertaining to these payments.

PENSION BENEFITS GUARANTEE CORPORATION (PBGC) Established under ERISA to ensure that pensions meet vesting obligations and to insure pensions should a plan terminate without sufficient funds to meet its vested obligation.

PENSION PLANS Plans that provide a fixed sum when employees reach a predetermined retirement age or when they no longer work due to disability.

PERCENTAGE CONTROL SYSTEM Wherein the cost of food or beverage is divided by sales to provide a percentage.

PERCEPTION OF VALUE A consumer's perception of what a product is worth.

PERPETUAL Continuous, endless.

PERPETUAL INVENTORY Accounting for inventory changes. Beginning and ending inventory figures are changed along with any sales or purchases.

PHYSICAL INVENTORY A count of all items on hand.

PIECEWORK The system of pay based on the number of items produced by each individual worker.

POINT-OF-SALE (POS) SYSTEM A sales transaction register and processor.

POPULARITY INDEX Total sales of an item divided by total number of that item sold.

PORTION One serving.

PORTION CONTROL Ensures that the correct amount is being served each time.

PORTION COST The cost of one serving.

PORTION SERVED The amount served to a customer.

PORTION SIZE A specific portion amount.

POSITION REPLACEMENT CARD A card prepared for each position in a company. Shows possible replacement candidates and their qualifications.

POTENTIAL COST Calculating what the expected cost of an item should be.

PPBSE Planning, programming, budgeting, staffing, and evaluating.

PRE-CHECKING SYSTEM Independent record of what is ordered from a kitchen.

PRE-COST/PRE-CONTROL Accounting system that determines what the food cost should be, compares it with the actual food cost, and includes sales analysis.

PREFERRED PROVIDER ORGANIZATIONS (PPOS) Groups of health-care providers that contract with employers, insurance companies, or third-party payers to provide medical care services at a reduced fee.

PREP YIELD PERCENTAGE The ratio of product yield after preparation to the quantity of product as purchased.

PRICE ELASTICITY The change in the rate of sales due to the change in price.

PRICE INDEXING Measures the effect of product price changes.

PRICE LOOK-UP (PLU) Assigned menu item numbers in POS systems.

PRIMAL CUT Primary division for cutting meat into smaller cuts.

PRIME COST The cost of a product after calculating and adding in labor.

PRINCIPAL Sum of money on which interest is paid.

PRIVILEGE CONTROL SYSTEM A system that permits or denies access to restricted areas.

PRO FORMA Statement prepared on the basis of anticipated results.

PROCEDURE The method of doing a task.

PRODUCT SPECIFICATION A listing of quality and service requirements necessary for products to be purchased from a vendor.

PRODUCTION SCHEDULE

The items and quantities that must be produced for a specific meal, day, etc.

PROFILE Data creating an outline of significant features.

PROFIT Gain.

PROPORTION The relationship between one thing and another with regard to size, number, or amount.

PROPRIETORSHIP Ownership.

PSYCHOGRAPHIC SEGMENTATION Segmentation based on lifestyles.

PURCHASE SPECIFICATIONS Standard requirements established for procuring items from suppliers.

PURVEYOR One who supplies provisions or food.

Q

QUALITY CONTROL Assuring the execution of tasks and responsibilities according to established standards.

QUANTITATIVE FORECASTING Forecasting based on past and present numerical data.

QUANTITATIVE METHODS Using numbers to help make decisions.

QUANTITY The amount; how much.

QUICK RATIO Current assets less inventory value, divided by current liabilities.

R

RANDOM WALK Assuming a present period of sales will be the same as a past period.

RANKING METHOD Ranks each job relative to all other jobs.

RATIO The ratio between two quantities is the number of times one contains the other; porportion.

RATIO ANALYSIS A technique for determining staff needs by using ratios between sales volume and the number of employees needed.

REACH Percentage of people in a target audience who will see or hear a specific advertising message.

RECEIPT A written statement that something has been received.

RECEIVING REPORT A report that indicates the value and quantity of items received.

RECIPE Directions used for preparing a menu item.

RECIPE COST The total cost of all ingredients in a recipe.

RECIPE YIELD The weight, count, or volume of food that a recipe will produce.

RECONSTITUTE Put back into original form, especially by rehydration.

RED-LINING Placing a red mark on a guest check so it cannot be used again.

REENGINEERING To change an enterprise to be more customer oriented or more efficient.

REPORT An account of facts used to give or get information.

REQUISITION To apply for something needed.

RESIDUAL INCOME ANALYSIS (RIA) Comparing the return on an investment to the cost of invested capital.

RETURN ON INVESTMENT A ratio found by dividing profit by investment.

REVENUE Income.

REVENUE CENTER Outlet or department that produces revenue.

RFP Request for proposal.

ROI (RETURN ON INVESTMENT) Incremental sales dollars divided by total costs.

ROP (RUN OF PAPER/RUN OF PRESS) Placement of advertisement anywhere within a publication that the publisher elects.

ROTATING MENU A menu that alternates in a series. Usually set up on a yearly basis.

S

SALARY A regular payment for services rendered.

SALES MIX The number of sales of individual menu items.

SALES REVENUE Money from the sale of certain items.

SCATTER PLOT Helps identify the relationship between two variables.

SEAT TURNOVER The number of times a seat is occupied during a meal period. Calculate by dividing the number of guests seated by the number of available seats.

SENSIBLE HEAT Heat measured by a thermometer.

SERVER BANKING When the server or bartender also does the cashier duties.

SHRINKAGE The amount of food lost due to cooking, dehydration, or theft.

SHRINKAGE (INVENTORY) The difference between what is on hand and what should be on hand.

SIMPLE RANKING SYSTEM Ranking jobs in order of difficulty or importance.

SIMPLIFY To make easier to understand or carry out.

SMART CARD A credit card with a computer chip that holds data.

SOCIAL APPROACH TO MANAGEMENT Considers management's responsibilities to employees, customers, and community as well as to its stockholders.

SOLO INSERT Usually printed on different stock than that used by the publication, this page is printed by the advertiser and inserted into a magazine or newspaper by the publisher.

SOLVENCY RATIOS Ratios that show an organization can meet its long-term debt obligations.

SPECIFICATION A detailed statement of the particulars of an item.

SPILLAGE The alcohol lost during the drink-making process.

SPOILAGE Loss due to poor food handling.

STAFF MANAGER The manager who assists and advises line managers.

STAGGERED SCHEDULING Scheduling employees to start and stop at different times according to the work pattern.

STAGGERED STAFFING Employees are staffed according to business volume.

STANDARD HOUR PLAN An employee is paid a basic hourly rate and an extra percentage of his or her base rate for production exceeding the standard.

STANDARD RECIPE Producing a particular food or drink item by a definite formula.

STANDARD-COST METHOD (BEVERAGE) Determines the cost of beverages from the number of each beverage sold, then compares it to the cost of beverage requisitions.

STANDARDIZE To make the same in size, shape, weight, quality, or quantity.

STANDARDIZED RECIPE Directions describing the way an establishment prepares a particular dish.

STANDARD-SALES METHOD (BEVERAGE) Comparing actual beverage sales with the sales value of the beverage.

STANDING ORDER An order for delivery that is automatic.

STATEMENT OF INCOME Shows whether an operation has made or lost money.

STATIC MENU A menu that rarely changes.

STEPPED COSTS Costs that increase in elongated steps but at regular intervals.

STOCK OPTION The right to purchase a stated number of shares in a company at today's price at a future time.

STOCKHOLDER The owner of stocks or shares in a company.

STOREROOM PURCHASES Items are placed into storage rather than sent to the kitchen.

STORES (FOOD COST) The value of food that is in storage.

STRAIGHT LINE METHOD Used when figuring depreciation on an item.

STRATEGIC CHANGE A change in a company's strategy, mission, or vision.

SUMMARIZE Briefly express, stating the main points.

SUNK COSTS Costs already incurred that cannot be recouped.

SYSTEM Components working together in the most efficient way.

T

TABLE D'HOTE A complete meal at a set price.

TARGET FOOD COST The amount a company hopes to spend for a particular menu item.

TENDER KEYS Cash register keys that break down sales by payment method.

THERM 100,000 Btu.

TIE-INS Joint venture promotions involving your company and another.

TIME AND MOTION STUDY A study done to establish a standard time for each job.

TIPPING FEE The cost of disposing of waste at a landfill.

TITLE VII OF THE 1964 CIVIL RIGHTS ACT States that an employer cannot discriminate on the basis of race, color, religion, sex, or national origin.

TOP-DOWN BUDGET A budget prepared by upper management and "passed on" to operating units.

TOTAL QUALITY MANAGEMENT (TQM) A program aimed at maximizing customer satisfaction through continuous improvements.

TRAINING Teaching new employees the basic skills needed to perform their jobs.

TREND ANALYSIS Study of a company's past employment needs over a time period of years to predict future needs.

TRIM The part or quantity of a product removed during preparation.

TRIPLICATE Three identical copies.

TUMBLE CHILL SYSTEM Pumpable foods prepared with steam kettles and then rapidly chilled.

U

UNIFORM PRODUCT CODE (UPC) A computer-readable code on a package.

UNIT Refers to the number or amount in a package.

UNIT COST The purchase price divided by the applicable unit.

U.S. SYSTEM The system of measurement used in the United States, whereby weight is measured in pounds and ounces, and volume is measured in cups and gallons.

USABLE PORTION The part of a fabricated product that has value.

USAGE METHOD (OF FOOD PURCHASING) Purchasing food based on past consumption.

V

VARIABLE COST The production cost that changes in direct proportion to sales volume.

VARIABLE EMPLOYEES Employees whose time requirements change with changes in business volume.

VARIABLE RATE Variable costs divided by sales.

VARIATION The extent to which a thing changes, or the change itself.

VENDOR The person or company who sells.

VERBALLY Expressed in words.

VERSATILE Easily changing or turning from one action to another.

VERTICAL Straight up and down.

VOLUME Calculated as length times width times height.

VOUCHER Evidence of payment in written form, such as a receipt.

W

WAGES The amount paid or received for work.

WEIGHT The measurement of mass or heaviness of an item.

WELL DRINK A drink not made with name-brand liquor.

WITHHOLDING TAX The deduction from a person's paycheck for the purpose of paying income taxes.

WORK SAMPLES Job tasks used in testing an applicant's performance.

WORK SIMPLIFICATION Finding the easiest and most productive way to perform a job or task.

WORKING CAPITAL The difference between current assets and current liabilities.

X

X MODE Allows reports to be produced on the POS register without resetting totals.

Y

YIELD The total created or the amount remaining after fabrication. The usable portion of a product.

YIELD CONVERSION FACTORS A factor that when multiplied by the gross weight amount of an item purchased shows how much will be available.

YIELD PERCENTAGE/ YIELD FACTOR The ratio of the usable amount to the amount purchased.

Z

Z MODE Produces final reports and clears information from a POS register.

ZERO-BASED BUDGET A budget prepared without previous budget figures.

Biography

Bill Wentz, upon graduating from The Cornell School of Hotel and Restaurant Management, began his career working in private clubs, most notably The Gaslight Club in Washington, D.C. Soon, an opportunity with ARA Services, a fast-growing food management firm now known as Aramark, opened the door that turned out to be a fulfilling and exciting 30-year career.

Starting as an assistant manager he rose through the ranks to food service director, district manager, regional operations manager and, finally, regional vice president, a position that he held for 15 years. During this period he was directly responsible for a wide variety of food service operations, including colleges, schools, office catering, industrial cafeterias, health care, senior services, and vending. Since leaving ARA Services he has been actively involved in assisting other food service enterprises with his expertise in management consulting and business development.

From this broad-based experience in the food service industry he has learned first hand many valuable insights as to what produces profitable businesses and sustains long-term satisfied customer and client relations. His knowledge and experience has been clearly written into this new book, *Food Service Management: How to Succeed in the High-Risk Restaurant Business — By Someone Who Did*, of which he is particularly proud. He welcomes the opportunity to share his knowledge about the many operational facets of the food service industry, such as how to get things done the right way, as well as down-to-earth advice about managing your time, your employees, and your future.

Bill and his wife Barbara now reside in Cincinnati, Ohio, and dedicate a large portion of their time to keeping up with their extended family of seven children and 11 grandchildren.

Index